Making
HANDBAGS

retro | chic | luxurious

Making
HANDBAGS

retro | chic | luxurious

ellen goldstein-lynch sarah mullins nicole malone

APPLE

Published in the UK in 2002 by
Apple Press
Sheridan House
112-116A Western Road
Hove
East Sussex BN# 1DD
UK

ISBN 1-84092-368-7

10 9 8 7 6 5 4 3 2 1

Interior & Cover Design: Rule29
Photography/Cover Image: Bobbie Bush Photography, www.bobbiebush.com
Project Manager/Copy Editor: Stacey Ann Follin
Technical Editor: Marya Amig
Proofreader: Karen Diamond

Printed in China

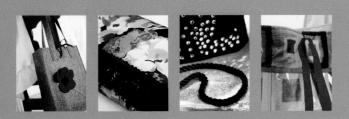

contents

introduction

Making Handbags is designed for anyone who has a passion for handbags—offering you a wonderful opportunity to create your own handbags with style and flair, to be the best-accessorized person in your neighborhood, and to be the envy of your friends and family. This book shows you, step by step, how to make four basic types of bags: a tote bag, a clutch bag, a drawstring bag, and a beach bag. The directions are easy to follow, the patterns concise and easy to read, and the projects fun to make. The book also includes a gallery of projects that shows you what you can achieve by building on the various projects in the book. What's more, it can serve as inspiration for your own designs.

Making Handbags offers perfect arts and crafts solutions for every occasion—from individual to group projects, to accessories for yourself and others. These projects make great group activities, so use them for Girl Scout troops or for students in the classroom. Don't forget holidays and birthdays; a handbag makes a super gift for that very special person. And is there a better way to spark up an outfit than with your own handbag creation?

This book will tickle your fancy and excite your creative mind. Get out your sewing machine, and dust it off. Sharpen your scissors. Pick your favorite fabrics, embellishments and trims, and flea-market hardware for your designs, and start sewing. Your wardrobe is waiting!

CHAPTER 1

basics

As Barbie has said time and time again, "Every morning, I wake up and thank God for my unique ability to accessorize!"

Accessories have been and continue to be the cornerstone of the fashion industry. If we can't afford to go out every season and buy a new, fashionable wardrobe, we go for the accessories. A handbag, a pair of shoes, a scarf, or a belt can easily update an outfit and give it a new look.

Accessories have played a major role in history. If it weren't for a simple drawstring pouch, Brutus would never have been able to conceal a dagger and slay Caesar. England wouldn't be England without the Queen Mother dressed in coordinated handbag, shoes, and hat. And the image of Jackie Kennedy in her gorgeous gowns wouldn't have had such a lasting impression had it not been for her accessories.

Also, movies and television have brought fashion and accessories to new heights. Watching Scarlett O'Hara in her beautiful dress, with her parasol, gloves, and handbag, walking among the injured in *Gone with the Wind* still remains a striking image. In the 1950s, every suburban housewife wanted to be like television's Donna Reed—stylishly dressed and perfectly accessorized.

Many accessories, besides being fashionable, are functional as well. We need handbags to hold our personal items, just as we need hats and shoes to protect us from the elements. Whether we're going to the beach or pool, carrying baby paraphernalia, going to work, or shopping, we usually bring an accessory along. Now perhaps we don't coordinate our handbags, shoes, and hats the same way we did in the 1930s, 1940s, and 1950s, and maybe the styles are different, but the demand for accessories remains constant.

But even today, handbags are an integral part of any accessory wardrobe. Throughout history, women have purchased bags in every size, shape, fabric, and color to accentuate their clothes. Although the look of these bags has changed over time, what remained a constant is the need for them to be fashionable. Bags with names like swagger, carpet, and feed have resurfaced with names like beach bag, tote, and drawstring. The clutch bag is now more contemporary, sporting a short shoulder strap or a wrist handle. Whereas yesterday's tote was strictly functional, today's tote is more about fashion.

So before you go to bed at night, or after you wake up in the morning, thank yourself for your ability to accessorize! And remember: Accessories are the name of the game. They're the spice of your wardrobe—and they're extensions of your personal style.

getting started

GATHERING ESSENTIAL TOOLS

You don't need a fully equipped sewing room or design studio to make wonderful handbags. All you need are a few basics and your imagination. You definitely need a **sewing machine**—the specific type doesn't matter, as long as you're comfortable with it. Whether you have the newest computerized model with embroidery capabilities or a 30-year-old workhorse, the machine should have a *reverse stitch selector* and *interchangeable presser foot attachments.* What's more, it should be well oiled and maintained. A sluggish machine is a hungry machine—and that type tends to "eat" the fabric.

Presser foot attachments are available for most machines. Some are necessary for basic sewing techniques—including the standard sewing foot, the zipper foot, and the satin stitch, or embroidery, foot. Others allow you to stitch buttonholes, attach binding, piece fabrics, and create decorative effects. So do your homework and make the investment. You never know when your imagination will call upon your "feet" to do the work.

Find a **clean, flat surface** to work on. A folding table, kitchen table, or sewing table is perfect. Make sure that the table is secure and doesn't wobble and that it's free from food and dirt, which could soil your creations. If you're working on the family dining room table, protect it with a pad or cutting board to keep it from getting damaged.

Lighting is crucial. Without proper lighting your eyes will play tricks on you. Natural light is best, but if you don't have the luxury of working in a room filled with windows, don't worry. Just make sure that you have sufficient light.

Work near a window or with the air conditioning on so you have **proper ventilation**, especially when you're working **craft or fabric glues**, which are essential for all handbag projects. Just make sure that your glue is less than 6 months old, and have an extra jar available as a backup.

To get the wrinkles out of any fabric, you're going to need an **iron**—and not just any iron but a good steam iron. So it's best to invest in a reliable model.

A craftsperson can never have too many pairs of **scissors**. You may want to have one pair for cutting fabric and another for cutting leather. Just make sure that your scissors are always sharp and that they fit comfortably in your hand. Many brands of ergonomically correct scissors are now available, so treat yourself to a pair. Rotary cutters are also great for cutting fabric, so you may want to have a pair of those as well. While we're on the cutting edge, don't forget sharp **pinking shears** for decorative detailing and sharp **utility and craft knives** for cutting leather. (The key word here is *sharp;* dull cutting tools won't even cut butter.) It's also a good idea to have a **steel or metal ruler** to use as a guide when cutting leather, to prevent injury.

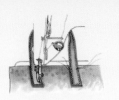

Another essential is strong **thread**, such as a polyester or polyester/cotton blend (whichever one works best on your machine). For some of the projects, you'll need contrasting colors, so stock up on your favorites.

Sewing machine needles are indispensable. Make sure that you have a range of different sizes for stitching different fabrics or for sewing with decorative threads. You'll also need to invest in a leather needle if you're sewing suede or leather. Besides your machine needles, **hand-sewing needles** are necessary for most projects, so make sure you have a variety of those on hand as well. For embroidery, use an embroidery needle; for beading on leather, use a Glover's needle; for lacing on leather, use a lacing needle; and for beading on fabric, use a quilting or beading needle. Also, change your needles regularly: Like scissors, they tend to get dull after constant use.

You'll need **straight pins** for pinning fabric, lining, and decorative trims in place. They come in various types and sizes. You can use whatever strikes your fancy, as long as you have enough of them.

Double-sided craft tape is great for turning under edges of fabric or temporarily adhering pieces of fabric before sewing. It's often better than glue because you don't run the risk of having glue seep into the fabric and stain it. Just as an electrician should never be without electrical tape, a craftsperson should never be without double-sided craft tape. Another handy type of tape is the old, reliable **masking tape**, which is useful for almost any craft project, especially when you're making handbags. So keep on hand several rolls in different widths.

Also, don't forget to have an ample supply of **fabric-marking pens and pencils**, including water- and air-soluble markers, for tracing patterns and marking fabrics.

Although some tools aren't essential to handbag making, they can certainly help make projects easier. Such optional tools include **snap- and grommet-setting kits**, a **hole punch**, **needle-nose pliers**, a small fine-toothed **handsaw** for cutting wood dowels, and a **loop turner**.

You now have the bare necessities for all your handbag-making projects. What are you waiting for? It's time to start making handbags with style!

selecting fabric

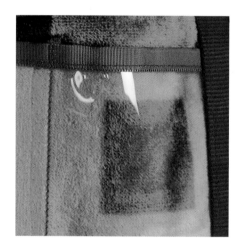

Fabric is usually the most prominent component of a handbag and, as such, it sets the tone for it. Your choice of fabric can coordinate or contrast with your outfit. It can allow you to be extravagant or conservative, elegant or frivolous. The fabrics you choose for your handbag, like the embellishments, reflect your imagination and your mood. So choose wisely. We've given you some examples of different types of fabrics that work well with our basic bag shapes, but don't limit yourself to these. As with everything else, be creative and experiment. The more skilled you become at making handbags, the more confident you'll be experimenting with less-traditional materials, such as lace, straw, and burlap.

When choosing a fabric for a project, determine the size of your bag, and choose the fabric and fabric width that's best suited to your project. Most fabrics suggested here can be used for any of the projects; however, some are easier to manipulate for the softer bags (such as the drawstring and clutch), whereas others work better for the sturdier bags (such as the tote and beach bag). Also, fabrics come in widths ranging from 30" to 60" (76 to 152 cm). Some fabrics—including cotton and cotton canvas, or cotton duck—should be washed and dried to preshrink them before working with them. Otherwise, you may run into problems if you get caught in the rain with your new bag. The key? Pick a fabric that's right for the handbag project you've selected.

Regardless of the fabric you choose, be sure to spray your handbag with a stain guard to protect the surface before you use it. If you need to clean your bag, do a test first. Try spot cleaning it with a soft, nonabrasive soap. You can also have your cloth bag dry cleaned. Use saddle soap on leather. If suede gets matted, use a suede brush to remove light dirt and to fluff up the nap.

Chintz

Chintz is a semiglazed, or shiny, printed cotton fabric that has a feminine, Victorian feel to it. It works as well as cotton and should be pretreated the same way—that is, it should be washed, dried, and ironed before you use it.

Corduroy

Defined as a soft, full-pile woven fabric with a lengthwise rib effect called wales, corduroy is a wonderful alternative to cotton. It comes in a wide range of colors and prints, and it has a three-dimensional look and feel to it. It also comes without the rib effect and as such has the look and feel of velvet. Like cotton, you should wash and dry corduroy before using it.

Cotton

Cotton is a great fabric to work with and is the number-one choice for handbag projects. It comes in various colors, prints, and textures, and you can even mix and match different cotton fabrics or create your own. Just remember to wash and dry the fabric first to preshrink it. Also, because this material tends to wrinkle, you'll want to iron it before you work with it.

Cotton Canvas or Cotton Duck

Cotton canvas, or cotton duck, is a woven cotton material that's considered one of the strongest and most durable of all cottons. It's used for awnings and boat covers, and it comes in a wide range of colors, prints, and weights. When making tote or beach bags, use #8 to #12 weight; when making fashion bags, use a #14 to #16 weight. Just remember to wash and dry the fabric first to preshrink it.

Quilted Cotton

Log cabin, around the world, and windowpane are all patchwork quilt designs that you can create and manipulate to form the body of a clutch, tote, or beach bag. First, piece and quilt the fabric, and then cut out the pattern pieces. If you don't want to use the quilted fabric for the entire bag, use parts of it for pockets or embellishments.

Denim

Denim is a durable twill woven fabric. It typically comes in indigo blue and is made of cotton or cotton-blend fibers. Popular for jeans and jackets, denim makes a wonderful fabric for all handbag projects in this book. Like cotton, denim should be washed and dried before you use it.

Faux Fur

Faux fur is made of acrylic fibers woven together to resemble animal fur. It would provide a fun look for any of the handbags in the book, either for the body of the bag or an accent. Just be careful when you cut and sew faux fur because it has a tendency to shed.

Leather and Suede

Leather and suede come from the skin of a calf, cow, goat, or pig. These fabrics are sold in various weights, so be sure to buy the appropriate weight for your type of bag: For a raw-edged bag, such as a tote or beach bag, purchase a heavier weight; for a clutch or drawstring bag, use a lighter weight. Suede is a finish that gives the leather a knobby texture. When selecting suede, you should also consider the weight of the skin. A heavier-weight skin may be too difficult to stitch into for a lighter-weight bag like a clutch bag, but it may be suitable for a tote bag.

When placing your patterns on fabric, you'll be working either with or against the grain. However, when you're working with suede or leather, you'll be placing the patterns around any imperfections on the skin. Make sure you buy a skin that's big enough to accommodate all the patterns, and try not to buy several small skins unless you match them by color and finish.

Linen

Linen is the oldest-known fabric available. It comes in various weights and colors and can be used for elegant day-bag designs like the clutch and drawstring bags. On the plus side, the fabric is strong, sturdy, and absorbent; on the minus side, it tends to wrinkle and can mildew easily. So don't use linen on a tote bag or beach bag that you're going to take to the beach or pool unless your lining is waterproof. Silk is a wonderful contrast fabric for linen.

Satin

Satin is a shiny, lustrous, woven fabric that is very delicate, has a tendency to snag, and is less durable than other fabrics. It comes in various colors and types: Peau de soie and satin crepe are two examples. Satin also can have an antique or aged look that would make a wonderful evening bag. Sateen is a variation of satin made from cotton, but it isn't as lustrous as the real thing.

Silk

Despite its fragile appearance, silk is one of the strongest natural fibers around. It's very flexible and absorbent, and it comes in a variety of vivid colors, rich jewel tones, and dramatic earth tones. The fabric works well with the clutch, drawstring, and tote bag patterns, and it begs to be decorated with fringe and tassels. For a more exotic, Far Eastern attitude and feel, you can create the look of raw silk by adding texture to traditional silk. Although silk is prone to water spots, they're temporary imperfections and can be removed by washing or dry cleaning.

Terry Cloth

Terry cloth is a highly absorbent, looped pile fabric that's woven or knitted. It's commonly used to make bath towels. Although it makes a durable fabric for a tote or beach bag, it can also make a statement as a drawstring bag or clutch.

Velvet

Velvet is made from cotton, rayon, or silk and has a soft, thick, luxurious surface. Crushed velvet appears wrinkled or ironed. Like corduroy, velvet comes in a wide range of colors and prints and would be ideal for any of the handbag projects in this book.

Vinyl

Vinyl, a plastic material with a leather-like appearance, comes in various colors, prints, and textures called embossing. It also comes in yardage that makes it easy to handle. Sometimes vinyl prints duplicate lizard, reptile, or snake skins. On the down side, vinyl can be difficult to sew because of its glossy finish, and it tends to slip or skip under the presser foot. To prevent this from happening, center 3" to 4" (7.5 to 10 cm) wide lengths of tear-away stabilizer on the seam line underneath the vinyl as you sew, using a Teflon presser foot.

Wool

Wool is a soft natural fiber that comes from the coat of a sheep. It's elastic, and it takes color well. It's water repellent, but it also absorbs water. It comes in solids, prints, and wonderful plaids, making it ideal for totes, clutches, and drawstring bags. You can even use this fabric for the beach bag pattern, as long as you don't use the bag as a beach bag. Just keep in mind that wool tends to shrink and deteriorate in sunlight, and it's a delicacy for moths.

embellishing your creation

Now for the pièce de resistance, the crème de la crème, the icing on the cake—a.k.a. the embellishments! Embellishments can either make or break your design. They add character to your creation by reflecting you and your personality.

Selecting the type of trim that's right for you is purely a matter of taste: Whatever suits your mood, goes great with your outfit, or makes the right statement is the appropriate trim to use. Just be diligent about your decision, be confident about your ideas, and most of all be creative. Embellishments are a way of expressing your inner self and should give you a sense of accomplishment. Just remember that the embellishments listed here are only suggestions. Use your imagination, and look around you for other things you can use to decorate your accessories. Let your creative juices flow, and think outside of the book. Here are some ideas to get you started.

Appliqués

Appliqués come in various sizes, shapes, and themes. Embroidered patches, flowers, and animals make great additions to the surface of your handbag, or they can be used to highlight a pocket. You can also use several small embroidered appliqués to create a story. While we're talking appliqué, don't forget reverse appliqué—that is, adding color to your bag through cutwork. This gives your creation a very personalized touch.

Bangles, Baubles, and Beads

You can never have enough of these little beauties! They come in every size, shape, and color. They can be hand sewn or glued to the bag or attached with a Be-Dazzler rhinestone setting machine or a handheld rhinestone setter. Use these little gems as accents, or use them to punctuate a fashion statement. Either way, they're sure to strike a brilliant chord.

Buttons

Buttons can be utilitarian when used as openings and closings for your bag, or they can be purely aesthetic when used as delightful accents. Use antique buttons, fancy buttons, big flat buttons, or clusters of buttons in a pattern. Any way you place them, buttons make a great accent.

Embroidery Stitches

Embroidery stitches—such as satin stitches, French knots, couching, and leaf stitches—add detailing to any style of bag. Use these decorative stitches by themselves or with embroidery appliqués or silk flowers for greater impact.

Eyelets, grommets, snaps, and studs

Eyelets, grommets, snaps, and studs can be used not only as functional embellishments but also as trims. Cover the entire front of the bag with grommets and eyelets for a military look. Or use snaps to attach appliqués that can be removed when you change your outfit.

Flowers

Handmade silk flowers, with that "picked straight from the garden" look, can add elegance and delicacy to any bag. Use one as a focal point on the flap or handle, or cluster a few (like a nosegay) for a bolder statement.

Fringe and Tassels

Fringe and tassels make great trims. They move when you do, so they're eye catchers. And they're fun to play with, so they add a bit of mischief to your creation.

Iron-on Transfers

Iron-on transfers can completely change the look of your fabric, or they can accentuate just a section of it. Either way, they can add a whimsical touch to your bag.

Jewelry

Use pieces of jewelry, such as necklaces and pins, to accent your bags. They can be permanent fixtures on the bag, or you can change them with your outfit or mood. It's always fun to go scavenging through flea markets and antique stores for just the right piece. And don't forget: Necklaces and bracelets make great handles as well.

Lace and Lace Appliqués

Add sophistication to your creation with a bit of lace and lace appliqué. Whether you select lace pieces, small lace flowers, or ruffled lace strips, the end result will be elegant.

Lanyards

Remember when you were a kid and you made lanyards to hold a whistle or key? Remember their vivid colors and intricately woven patterns? Add a splash of color and some nostalgia to your handbag creation by using those lanyard laces as a trim or handle.

Fabric Paint

Use fabric paint to add a bit of whimsy to your bags. This embellishment is perfect for young children who enjoy being creative. Just make sure you have a variety of colors available, then sit back and let the creativity flow.

Quilting and Smocking

Although quilting and smocking are techniques rather than trims, they can add another dimension to your bags. You can buy pieces of ribbon and lace that have already been smocked and use them as decoration, or you can quilt a patch of your own and use it as a signature pocket. That will get heads turning for sure!

Ribbons

Ribbons make fabulous accents as decorations or drawstrings. Try making ribbon flowers, buds, and leaves on a flap or pocket. Or use several lengths, types, and colors, and weave them for greater impact.

Rope

For a nautical or outdoorsy feel, use rope as a drawstring, handle, or trim. Rope adds a feeling of salt air and the rugged outdoors to just about any bag you choose. If you like the rope idea but want a more sophisticated look, use satin cording or satin braid, which comes in various colors and sizes.

Sequins

Sequins add sparkle and pizzazz to any creation. Make sure to have a variety of colors on hand. Experiment with creating a picture or just use them as accents.

Topstitching

Topstitching, like embroidery stitches, adds detailing interest to your bag. Use a contrasting color thread when topstitching for a great accent to any bag.

understanding the terminology

For readers who have never used a pattern or sewn before, don't panic: Making your own handbags can be fun, rewarding, and as easy as 1-2-3. The key to success is reading and understanding the patterns, following the instructions, and knowing the language.

The questions and answers below will help familiarize you with the basics—that is, what you need to know before you tackle your first handbag project. Whether you're a novice or a pro, it can't hurt to review.

USING PATTERNS

What is a pattern?

A pattern is a template that you'll use to create a handbag. Each component of the bag has a separate pattern piece—for example, the front and back piece, the handle, and the gusset. Make sure you have all pattern pieces (in the appropriate size) before you start your project.

What are pattern markings?

Pattern markings (such as pocket placement markings, notches for matching pieces of the bag, and seam allowance guides) are guideposts on the patterns to help you to assemble your handbag. These markings should be transferred from the pattern to the fabric using a chalk pencil, a tracing wheel and dressmaker's carbon paper, or a water- or air-soluble marking pen.

What is the center front and center back?

The center front and center back are the lines on a pattern that indicate the middle of the front and back sections of the bag.

What are notches?

Notches are tiny V-shaped markings that appear on the outside edges of the pattern. They act as signposts to ensure that all pattern pieces are properly aligned. If they aren't, your finished bag will look lopsided.

What is a seam?

A seam is the point where two or more edges of material are held together by stitches.

What is seam allowance?

Seam allowance is the amount of fabric between the stitching line and the edge of the fabric. For all projects in this book, ⅜" (1 cm) is the recommended seam allowance unless otherwise noted.

What is a gusset?

A gusset is an insert in the side seam of a bag that gives depth and expansion to the bag.

What is interfacing?

Interfacing is a fabric that's placed between the outside fabric and the lining to add support and strength to the bag. In most of the projects, fusible interfacing is recommended.

What is lining?

Lining is generally a lighter-weight fabric used for the inside of the bag. It can be the same color as the outside of the bag or a contrasting color for more visual interest.

What is a loop turner?

A loop turner is a metal tool about 10" (25.5 cm) long with a latch at the end that's used to turn bias tubing right side out or lace a drawstring through a narrow tube of fabric.

What is the selvage?

Either of the two finished edges of the fabric is the selvage.

What is the grain?

The grain is the way the threads or knit ribs run on the fabric, either straight or lengthwise, parallel to the selvage, or crosswise, between the selvages. Fabric is more stable on the straight or lengthwise grain.

What is bias?

A line that runs diagonally across the grain of the fabric is known as the bias. Cutting fabric on the bias adds maximum stretch to the material.

What is pinking?

Pinking is cutting a serrated or V-shaped edge using pinking shears. This is a decorative edge treatment that can be applied to felt and leather. If you decide to pink other materials, just keep in mind that pinked material will fray.

What is piping?

Piping is a narrow strip of fabric that's cut on the bias, folded in half, and used to trim handbags. The fabric often is filled with a narrow piece of cording to give the piping dimension.

KNOWING THE BASIC STITCHES

Several types of stitching are used throughout the handbag projects. Some terms may be familiar, others may not.

What are basting stitches?

Basting stitches are long stitches used to temporarily hold fabric pieces together. Most basting is done by hand, but some machines have basting stitches, so check out your machine before you begin.

What are box stitches?

Box stitches are formed by machine sewing a rectangular box and then sewing an X inside the box. This stitching is used to attach handbag handles securely.

What is tacking?

Tacking is used to sew one section of a bag to another, using a few tight stitches.

What is topstitching?

Topstitching is a decorative type of stitching that's done on the outside of the bag. It can be one or two rows of machine stitching in the same or a contrasting color.

Now you truly are a pro: You've mastered the basic key terms and stitch types, and you're ready to begin. So gather your essential tools, and let's get started!

CHAPTER 2

making tote bags

A tote, or shopping, bag should be the most versatile bag in your collection. It's an all-purpose carryall, designed for easy access and storage. Tote bags were probably the earliest bags designed for practical use: Our ancestors used them to carry their food and necessities from one cave to another. But times have changed, and so have tote bags. Nowadays, they're fashionable as well as useful. Totes can be made with various fabrics plus exotic leathers, furs, and plastics. They can be large or small, with or without pockets. Totes can accommodate a notebook, an umbrella, cosmetics, or anything else a woman on the go might wish to carry. They're perfect as a second bag for travel or in place of a briefcase or portfolio. But why stop there? A tote, in the right design, with brilliance and sparkle, can be a stunning evening accessory.

The basic construction is simple: Most totes feature a front and back panel, with a gusset in between that gives the bag depth, along with two straps or handles. Just modify the basic pieces to create a bag or two in the perfect size and style for you.

flower appliquéd tote

Everyone loves flowers—especially when they're attached to a stylish handbag like this one. The shape lends itself to various fabrics, colors, and trims, making this tote perfect for any occasion. Here, a soft gray felt makes an elegant yet casual statement. Use leather or vinyl in dark, muted colors, and this bag would be perfect for business, or use bright colors to make it a fun accessory for weekend trips. So add your own personal trims and touches, and spruce up your collection with this innovative tote. This bag makes an excellent project for all ages.

MATERIALS
- 24" × 24" (61 cm × 61 cm) piece of gray felt
- 6" × 24" (15 cm × 61 cm) piece of green felt
- 6" × 10" (15 cm × 25.5 cm) piece of red felt
- 3" (7.5 cm) length of black fringe trim

TOOLS
- Sewing machine
- Matching thread
- Pins
- Hand-sewing needle
- Scissors
- Pinking shears
- Water-soluble marking pen
- Iron

GETTING STARTED
- Press the felt to remove any wrinkles.
- Enlarge and trace the Tote Bag Front/Back, Bottom/Gusset, and Handle patterns onto the gray felt, using the water-soluble marking pen and following the instructions on the pattern pieces. Trace two Handles onto the green felt. Trace one Tote Bag Flower Appliqué Stem onto the green felt and five Flower Petals onto the red felt.
- Transfer all placement locations for the handles, tie closure, flower, stem, and center bottom from the patterns onto the felt using the water-soluble marking pen.
- Using the scissors, cut the front, back, bottom and gusset pieces, stem, flower petals, and two green handles from the felt. Cut two 8" × ¼" (20.5 cm × 0.6 cm) pieces of red felt for the tie closure.
- Using the pinking shears, cut out the two gray handles.

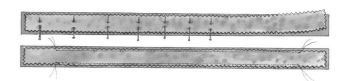

step 1 Pin each pinked gray handle on top of a green handle. Topstitch ⅛" (0.3 cm) from the raw edges, starting and stopping 2" (5 cm) from the short ends.

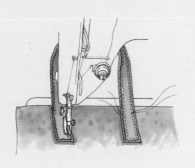

step 2

Topstitch the handles onto the tote front and back at the handle placement markings transferred from the pattern. Machine tack the tie closure pieces to the front and back centered between the handles, ¼" (0.6 cm) from the top edge.

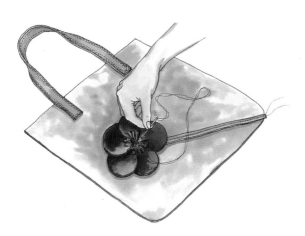

step 3 Topstitch the flower stem onto the right side of the tote front. Hand stitch the flower petals onto the right side of the front, overlapping the petals like a fan. Finish the center of the flower by rolling up the 3" (7.5 cm) length of black fringe trim and hand stitching it in place.

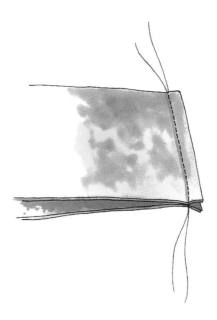

step 4 With right sides together, stitch the bottom and gusset pieces together using ⅜" (1 cm) seam allowance. Topstitch the seam open on the right side, ⅛" (0.3 cm) from both sides of the center bottom seam.

tips> When choosing a fabric for this bag, select one that doesn't fray along its raw edges, such as vinyl, plastic, or leather. To embellish the flower, add leaves, rhinestones, or more flowers, or cut the petals with a decorative edge.

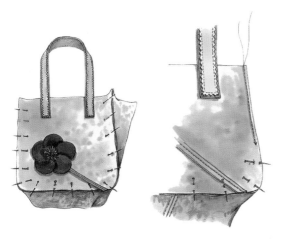

step 5 With wrong sides together, pin the bottom and gusset pieces to the tote front, matching the top edges and the center bottom. On the front, topstitch ⅛" (0.3 cm) from the raw edge. Repeat this step to attach the bottom and gusset pieces to the tote back. Following the manufacturer's instructions, remove any visible marks from the water-soluble marking pen.

reversible denim tote bag

Denim is one of the few fabrics that really lends itself to casual outdoor living. Its comfortable feel, easygoing look, and laid-back "attitude" are captured in this reversible tote bag. Using pockets from jeans and decorative studs, you can create your own designer look. But don't just stop with one: Denim bags are great in multiples and in different sizes. What's more, this project is lots of fun for kids.

MATERIALS

- 36" × 48" (91.5 cm × 122 cm) piece of denim
- 4 yards (366 cm) of cording with ⅜" (1 cm) seam allowance
- Decorative studs

TOOLS

- Sewing machine
- Zipper foot for sewing machine
- Contrasting thread
- Pins
- Hand-sewing needle
- Scissors
- Water- or air-soluble marking pen
- Iron
- Loop turner
- Stud-setting tool

GETTING STARTED

- Press the denim fabric to remove any wrinkles.
- Enlarge and trace the Tote Bag Front/Back, Bottom/Gusset, and Reversible Denim Tote Bag Pocket patterns onto the denim, following the instructions on the pattern pieces and using the water- or air-soluble marking pen. Transfer all pattern markings. Trace the Tote Bag Handle pattern, following the instructions on the pattern piece and adding ⅜" (1 cm) seam allowance to both long edges of the handle so you have four pieces that measure 1¾" × 24" (4.5 cm × 61 cm).
- Cut out all pieces.

1   Following the fold lines, turn the edges of one pocket to the wrong side and press. Topstitch the pocket ⅛" (0.3 cm) from the top edge on top of the double fold. Topstitch ⅜" (1 cm) from the top edge of the pocket if double stitching is desired. Using the stud-setting tool and following the manufacturer's instructions, set the studs on the markings on the front of the pocket.

2   Pin the pocket to the center of the outside front, 3" (7.5 cm) down from the top edge. Topstitch ⅛" (0.3 cm) from the edge around the sides and bottom of the pocket. Topstitch ⅜" (1 cm) from the side and bottom edges of the pocket if double stitching is desired.

3   Pin the cording to the outside front and back pieces, beginning and ending the piping ¾" (2 cm) from the top edge to reduce bulk in the seam. Hand baste the cording in place within the seam allowance.

4   With right sides together, sew the outside bottom and gusset pieces at the center bottom using ⅜" (1 cm) seam allowance. Topstitch the seam open on the right side of the denim, ⅛" (0.3 cm) from both sides of the center bottom seam.

5   Pin the outside bottom and gusset pieces to the outside front with right sides together, and match the top edges and center bottom. Attach the zipper foot to your sewing machine, and stitch as close as possible to the cording.

6   Repeat Step 5, pinning and stitching the bottom and gusset pieces to the outside back.

7   Repeat Steps 1 through 5, using the wrong side of the denim as the right side of the lining.

8   With right sides together, stitch the handles together using ⅜" (1 cm) seam allowance. Turn the handles right side out using the loop turner. Press the handles. Topstitch the handles ⅛" (0.3 cm) from the edges. Topstitch the handles ⅜" (1 cm) from the edges if double stitching is desired.

9   Hand baste the handles to the outside front and back, matching the raw edge of the handles with the raw edge of the top. Make sure right sides are together and within the ⅜" (1 cm) seam allowance.

10 With right sides together, place the lining inside the exterior of the tote, and pin the two layers together. Make sure the handles are tucked inside, between the inside and outside lining. Stitch around the top using ⅜" (1 cm) seam allowance and leaving a 6" (15 cm) opening to turn the bag right side out. (*Note:* The right side of the lining is the wrong side of the denim.)

11 Turn the bag right side out. Turn the seam allowances to the inside along the opening, and pin the opening closed. To finish the bag, topstitch ⅛" (0.3 cm) around the top edge, closing the opening. Following the manufacturer's instructions, remove any visible marks from the water- or air-soluble marking pen.

tips

Make your own piping by cutting a 1⅛" (2.8 cm) bias strip of denim and gluing or stitching ⅛" (0.3 cm) cording inside; just make sure the seam allowance of the cording equals ⅜" (1 cm). Also, consider embellishing a pocket from an old pair of jeans with beads, rhinestones, or fabric paint and using the same decoration on the front of the bag.

mini bridal tote bag

MATERIALS

- 18" × 18" (45.5 cm × 45.5 cm) piece of white bridal satin for outside
- 13" × 12" (33 cm × 30.5 cm) piece of lining fabric
- 13" × 12" (33 cm × 30.5 cm) piece of fusible interfacing
- 12" × 7" (30.5 cm × 18 cm) piece of felt or quilt batting
- 6 ½ yards (594 cm) of ⅛" (0.3 cm) wide satin ribbon
- 13" (33 cm) of ⅜" (1 cm) wide white braided trim
- 26" (66 cm) of ½" (1.3 cm) wide organza ribbon
- 1 white satin rosebud
- 4 pearl beads
- 2 beaded leaf appliqués
- Two 18" (45.5 cm) lengths of ⅛" (0.3 cm) wide cording

TOOLS

- Sewing machine
- Zipper foot for sewing machine
- Matching thread
- Pins
- Hand-sewing needle
- Scissors
- Air-soluble marking pen
- Iron
- Double-sided craft tape
- Adhesive tape
- Craft glue

GETTING STARTED

- Use the Mini Bridal Tote Bag pattern.
- Press the fabrics to remove any wrinkles.
- Press the fusible interfacing to the wrong side of the satin fabric.
- Using the air-soluble marking pen, trace the Mini Bridal Tote Bag Front/Back and Bottom/Gusset patterns onto the satin and the lining fabric, following the instructions on the pattern pieces.
- Using the air-soluble marking pen, transfer the ribbon, bead, and rosebud placement markings to the satin front.
- Using the air-soluble marking pen, trace the Mini Bridal Tote Bag Front/Back patterns onto the felt or quilt batting, following the instructions on the pattern pieces and eliminating the top ⅜" (1 cm) turn-in allowance.
- Cut out all pieces.
- Cut two 5" (12.5 cm), two 6" (15 cm), and two 7" (18 cm) pieces of satin ribbon. Cut two 6" (15 cm) and two 7" (18 cm) pieces of organza ribbon. Cut one 6" (15 cm) and one 7" (18 cm) piece of braided trim. Cut the remaining satin ribbon into six equal pieces.

Here comes the bride, all dressed in white, from her veil to her beautiful, delicate mini tote bag. Made of woven satin and organza ribbons and trimmed with a rosebud flower and leaf appliqué, this bag captures the romantic mood of a wedding day. It's ideal for carrying the bride's personal items, or even cards from guests.

But this mini tote bag doesn't have to be just for weddings. Using black, navy, or burgundy woven satin ribbons, or different-colored organza and satin ribbons, you can create your own special evening bag.

1 Lightly glue the felt or quilt batting to the wrong side of the satin front and back, placing the top edge of the felt ⅜" (1 cm) below the raw edge of the satin fabric. Turn the top edge of the satin front to the wrong side onto the felt, and glue it in place.

2 Using the double-sided craft tape, place the 7" (18 cm) vertical ribbons. Trim along the top edge of the tote front as noted on the Mini Bridal Tote Bag Front/Back pattern, and then place the 6" (15 cm) horizontal ribbons and braided trim on the left side of the tote front. Weave the ribbons and trim over and under each other until they're all woven.

3 Using the double-sided craft tape, tape down the ribbon edges to the right side and the bottom of the tote front. Machine stitch the ribbons and braided trim to the fabric about ⅛" (0.3 cm) from the edges to keep them in place.

4 With right sides together, sew the outside bottom and gusset pieces at the center bottom using ⅜" (1 cm) seam allowance.

5 Repeat Step 4 to join the bottom and gusset pieces of the lining.

6 Using the double-sided craft tape, tape the top ⅜" (1 cm) turn-in allowance to the wrong side on the lining front and back.

7 Hand stitch the pearl beads and rosebud to the front of the bag as noted on the Mini Bridal Tote Bag Front/Back pattern.

8 To make the cording, cut two 1⅛" × 18" (2.8 cm × 45.5 cm) bias strips of satin. Fold the strips in half lengthwise with wrong sides together, and glue the cording in the center. Pin the cording around the sides and bottom of the satin front and back, matching the raw edges and leaving a little extra cording at the top edges. Hand baste the cording in place. Machine stitch the cording to the tote front and back using a zipper foot. Be sure to start and stop sewing where noted on the pattern.

9 With right sides together, baste the bottom and gusset pieces around the satin front and back, and then pull the cording ends out of the seams where they're attached. Using a zipper foot, machine stitch as close as possible to the cording around the sides and bottom of the bag. Turn the bag right side out. Check to see that the cording starts evenly ⅜" (1 cm) from the top edge. Sew lining bottom and gusset pieces around front and back lining pieces.

10 Take three of the remaining lengths of satin ribbon, secure the ends with the adhesive tape and braid them together, and secure the ends with another piece of tape. Repeat for the other three lengths of satin ribbon. Using the double-sided craft tape, secure the braided ribbons inside the bag where you want the handles to go.

11 Take the two 5" (12.5 cm) lengths of ribbon, and knot each of the four ends. Using the double-sided craft tape, secure one end of each ribbon inside the bag at the center front and the center back.

12 Drop the lining into the bag. Match the folded edges, securing them together with the double-sided craft tape, and then topstitch around the top of the bag ⅛" (0.3 cm) from the edge.

13 Using the craft glue and following the placement guide on the Mini Bridal Tote Bag Front/Back pattern, attach the two leaf appliqués to the front of the tote. Tie the ribbon closures together in a small bow.

tip

Experiment with ribbons of varying widths, colors, and textures for countless new looks.

edge-laced leather tote bag

MATERIALS

- 33" × 20" (84 cm × 51 cm) piece of medium-weight leather skin
- Three 2-yard (183 cm) lengths of leather lacing

TOOLS

- Lacing needle
- Scissors
- Leather hole puncher
- Utility or craft knife
- Steel ruler
- Awl or pushpin
- Cutting mat or surface
- Craft glue or rubber cement
- Pattern weights

GETTING STARTED

- Enlarge and cut out the Edge-Laced Leather Tote Bag Front/Back and Bottom/Gusset patterns, following the instructions on the pattern pieces. Cut out the Edge-Laced Leather Tote Bag Flap and Button patterns.
- Cut two 27" × 1" (68.5 cm × 2.5 cm) strips of leather for the handles.
- Place the pattern pieces on top of the leather and pattern weights on top of the pattern, line up the steel ruler along the straight edges of the patterns, and cut the leather with the utility or craft knife. Let the edge of ruler guide the knife as you cut. When cutting rounded edges, simply use the edge of your pattern as guide. Be sure to cut on a proper surface.
- Using the awl or pushpin, transfer the handle placement markings from the Front/Back pattern to the top edges of the front and back by poking the points through the leather. Stitching lines may be lightly scratched into the surface of the leather. Then transfer the hole markings to the front and back and the bottom and gusset pieces with the awl or pushpin.

This bag captures a bit of sixties history—but don't think that by wearing the bag you're out of style: Lace, topstitching, embroidery, and appliqué are the rage of the "new generation." So go ahead and use leather and leather lacing, or experiment with vinyl and lanyard laces or extra-long shoelaces. Try using different types of lacing techniques for a totally unique look, and have a blast!

1 Punch out all holes according to the pattern markings using the leather hole puncher.

2 Insert one leather lace into the lacing needle, make a knot at one end, and whipstitch the front of the bag to the bottom and gusset pieces. After the stitching is complete, tie a knot to secure the top corner of the front to the gusset corner. Repeat this step to attach the back to the bottom and gusset pieces.

3 Insert another leather lace into the lacing needle and, using a running stitch, stitch the wrong side of the flap to the right side of the back of bag. Start stitching from inside the bag, one hole over from the center back of the flap, leaving a 2" (5 cm) tail. After you've stitched the back of the bag to the flap, continue the running stitch on just the flap, around to the center-front stitch. At the center-front stitch, leave enough extra lacing to form a loop. (This loop will later secure to a rolled-leather button on the front of the bag.) Continue lacing around the flap and again securing the back of the bag to the flap until you're back where you started. Leave a 2" (5 cm) tail at the end of lacing, and cut. Secure the ends of lacing on the inside of the back of the bag by tying the 2" (5 cm) tails together.

4 To create a rolled-leather button, apply the craft glue or rubber cement down the center of the leather button piece to about 2" (5 cm) from the pointed end. From the wide end, and with the right side out, roll the leather tightly, stretching the pointed tail and keeping the tip centered. Stop rolling when you get to the last 1½" (4 cm) of the tail. Punch a hole in the center of the entire roll. Pull the tail end of the button through the hole, and pull tightly. After the pointed end is pulled through the hole, split the tail in half with the utility or craft knife.

5 Insert the two pointed ends of the button into the holes in the front of the bag. Tie the ends together inside the bag to secure the button in place.

6 Insert the last leather lace into the lacing needle, and attach the handles to the front and back of the bag with a box stitch. Start lacing from the inside of the bag, leaving a tail and tying the ends together on the inside to secure.

tips

When choosing a fabric for this bag, select any durable material that doesn't fray along its raw edges—such as UltraSuede or vinyl. Also, you can use lanyard laces, yarn, or other thin trims for the lacing, and you can experiment with different edge-lacing techniques.

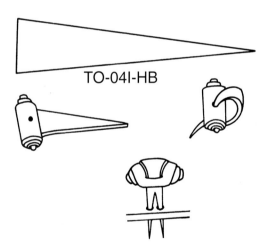

TO-04I-HB

CHAPTER 3

making clutch bags

Defined as a small usually strapless handbag, the *clutch bag* gained popularity in the 1950s as a major fashion statement. Starlets of the silver screen such as Marilyn Monroe and Rita Hayworth carried variations of this bag in different fabrics and leathers. Today, clutch bags can be seen in every shape and size, from the classic envelope to the expandable accordion, with or without straps and ornamentation. Although the clutch bag may not be the most secure bag in your collection, it's without a doubt a stylish companion to any outfit.

So use your imagination to create clutch bags with your own personalized styles and designs. After all, they're easy to make: You simply use a one-piece front and back, with gussets for stability and expansion. Adding embellishments or using vintage fabrics adds character to this classic style of bag. By following our lead, your clutch bag can be very chic, very retro, and very now.

fringed silk clutch bag

Elegant and sophisticated, fun and funky, this classic bag can be incorporated into your wardrobe for just about any occasion. Use your imagination to create a great daytime and playtime bag using ginghams, cotton prints, or canvas. Or dress the bag up with satins, chintz, or silk. And don't skimp on your trims. Whether it's fringe, flowers, bows, or rhinestones, the embellishments will add the personal charm.

MATERIALS

- 15" × 15" (38 cm × 38 cm) piece of fabric for outside
- 15" × 15" (38 cm × 38 cm) piece of lining fabric
- 15" × 15" (38 cm × 38 cm) Pellon or thin quilting batting
- 8" (20.5 cm) length of hook-and-loop fastener ($\frac{3}{4}$" [2 cm] wide)
- 10" (25.5 cm) fringe trim

TOOLS

- Sewing machine
- Thread
- Hand-sewing needle
- Scissors
- Fabric marking pen or pencil
- Iron

GETTING STARTED

- Press fabric to remove any wrinkles.
- Trace Clutch Bag Front/Back and Gusset patterns onto the outside fabric, lining fabric, and batting, following the instructions on the pattern pieces.
- Transfer fastener markings to appropriate pieces.
- Cut out all pieces.

step 1
Baste all batting pieces to the wrong side of all outside fabric pieces all around the edges within the ⅜" (I cm) seam allowance.

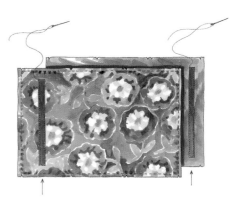

step 2
Hand stitch the hook part of the fastener to the outside front. Hand stitch the loop part of the fastener to the lining flap. (*Note*: The placement of the hook and loop prevents the fringe from getting caught in the hook.)

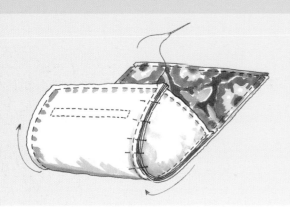

step 3

Baste gussets around the edge of both the front and back flap pieces, right sides facing each other. Be sure to match up all the notches. Machine stitch the gussets to the front, back, and flap pieces at ⅜" (I cm) seam allowance. To prevent the inner corner of the fabric from puckering later, don't stitch the top ⅜" (I cm) of the gusset to where it meets the flap.

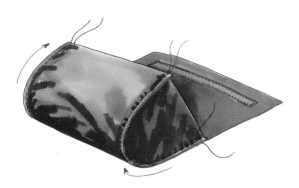

step 4
Repeat Step 3 for lining pieces.

step 5
Place lining inside of outside fabric with right sides facing each other, matching all seams.

step 6 Baste and then stitch the lining and outside fabric together all around the outer edge at ⅜" (I cm) seam allowance, leaving a small opening for turning at the center front section. Clip off excess bulk on the flap corners. Turn the bag right side out through the opening. Press seams flat with an iron.

step 7 Top stitch at ⅛" (0.3 cm) all around the edge of the bag. The topstitch will close the opening in the center front of the bag.

tips > This bag can be made with any material. Get creative: Use chintz, decorative cottons, or velvet, and match all your latest clothing purchases. Use a variety of trims to complement your fabric selections or enhance your wardrobe.

step 8 Tack stitch the top corners of the gussets flat so that the gussets will fold into the bag when it is closed.

step 9 Stitch the fringe trim to the bottom edge of the flap, turning under ½" (I.3 cm) on both ends to prevent fraying.

iron-on transfer with sequins and beads clutch bag

Iron-on images aren't just for T-shirts anymore. Using a personal computer and the Clutch Bag pattern, you can transform your favorite pictures, original designs, or pet photos into a unique handbag. Jazz it up with sequins and beads, fringe, or tassels, and you'll be a showstopper wherever you go.

MATERIALS

- 17" × 15" (43 cm × 38 cm) piece of canvas fabric
- 15" × 15" (38 cm × 38 cm) piece of lining fabric
- 8" (20.5 cm) length of ¾" (2 cm) wide hook-and-loop fastener
- 1 small package of sequins
- 1 small package of small beads

TOOLS

- Sewing machine
- Matching thread
- Hand-sewing needle
- Beading needle
- Scissors
- Fabric-marking pen or pencil
- Iron
- Iron-on transfer paper for computer printer
- Computer with printer
- Fabric glue

GETTING STARTED

- Find some images you would like to have on your handbag. They can be personal pictures from a digital camera or images or photos scanned into your computer or downloaded from the Internet.
- Print the images onto the iron-on transfer paper, following the manufacturer's instructions. Then press the fabric with the iron. Iron the printed transfer paper to the canvas, following the manufacturer's instructions.
- For variation, cut out around different shapes and place them all over the fabric, or print the same image twice and print one on the flap and one on the front of bag, positioning each so that they match up when the bag is closed. Just keep in mind the shape of the bag without the seam allowances and how it will look when it's sewn together.

1 Trace the Clutch Bag Front/Back and Gusset patterns onto the outside fabric and lining fabric. Transfer closure markings to the clutch bag body using the fabric-marking pen or pencil. Cut out all pieces.

2 Create a loop handle by cutting a piece of the canvas 14" × 1" (35.5 cm × 2.5 cm). Fold the two long edges of the handle ⅜" (1 cm) to the wrong side, and press and glue them in place. Then fold the long edges in half again, matching the previously folded edges, and press and glue in place. Topstitch the handle along both long sides ⅛" (0.3 cm) from the edge.

3 Embellish the images printed on the fabric with hand-sewn sequins and beads. An easy way to do this is to bring the needle and thread up through fabric, string one sequin and one bead and then go back through the hole in the sequin and back into the fabric in the same spot that you entered. The bead acts as a stopper and holds the sequin in place.

4 Hand stitch the loop part of the hook-and-loop fastener to the outside front, following the placement markings. Hand stitch the hook part of the fastener to the lining flap.

5 Hand baste the gussets to the edge of both the front and back of the clutch body, with right sides together and the notches matching. Machine stitch the gussets to the front and back of the clutch body with ⅜" (1 cm) seam allowance. To prevent the inner corner of the fabric from puckering later, don't stitch the top ⅜" (1 cm) of the gusset where it meets the flap.

6 Repeat Step 5 for the lining.

7 Place the lining inside the outside of the clutch body with right sides together and match all seams. Also, insert the handle where the top of the flap is when the bag is closed. The handle should be placed between the canvas fabric and the lining, with the loop positioned inside both layers and the raw edge of handle meeting the raw edges of the outside and lining fabrics.

8 Hand baste and then machine stitch the lining and outside fabric together around the outer edge, using ⅜" (1 cm) seam allowance and leaving a small opening for turning at the center front. Be sure to catch the handle in the stitching. Clip off any excess bulk on the flap corners.

9 Turn the bag right side out through the opening. Press the seams flat with the iron, being careful not to press the transfer and beaded areas.

10 Topstitch at ⅛" (0.3 cm) around the edges of the bag, making sure to close the opening at the center of the bag.

11 Tack the top corners of the gussets flat so they'll fold into the bag when it's closed. You can add a sequined embellishment here, if you like.

faux fur clutch bag

"Lions, Tigers and Bears, oh my!" Even Dorothy would be thrilled to carry this faux fur clutch bag. The flap has been modified with a point, to put you in the right direction. This bag makes an excellent fashion statement, whether it's in the Emerald City or back in Kansas. So experiment with different types of faux furs, and create your own collection of fuzzy friends.

MATERIALS

- 15" × 15" (38 cm × 38 cm) piece of faux fur fabric
- 15" × 15" (38 cm × 38 cm) piece of lining fabric
- 15" × 15" (38 cm × 38 cm) piece of Pellon or thin quilt batting
- 1 snap set

TOOLS

- Sewing machine
- Matching thread
- Hand-sewing needle
- Scissors
- Fabric-marking pen or pencil
- Iron
- Snap-setting kit

GETTING STARTED

- To create the pointed flap, modify the Clutch Bag Front/Back pattern according to the following steps: First, measure and mark the center of the flap at the top edge of the flap section, and then measure and mark 2" (5 cm) down from the flap corners along both edges of the flap section. Then, cut from the center mark to the 2" (5 cm) marks in each direction; the ⅜" (1 cm) seam allowance will now follow this shape. For the snap, measure and mark 1⅜" (3.5 cm) down from the flap point (for the ball section) and 2⅜" (6 cm) up from the edge in the center of the front section (for the socket section).
- Press the lining fabric to remove any wrinkles.
- Trace the Front/Back and Clutch Bag Gusset patterns onto the faux fur, the lining fabric, and the Pellon or quilt batting, but don't mark hook-and-loop closure locations.
- Cut out all pieces.

1 Follow Steps 1 through 8 of the Fringed Silk Clutch Bag project, eliminating Step 2.

2 Topstitch at ⅛" (0.3 cm) around the gussets and the front of the bag only. The topstitching will close the opening at the center of the bag.

3 Tack the top corners of the gussets flat so they'll fold into the bag when it's closed.

4 Using the snap-setting kit, attach the snap at the markings on the flap and front, following the manufacturer's instructions.

tips

For a slight variation, try modifying the flap by rounding the corners or making it asymmetrical, but avoid cutting beyond the 2" (5 cm) mark, or the flap will be too short to cover the front. You can also experiment with different fasteners to close the bag, such as buttons and magnetic snaps.

ultrasuede clutch bag

Soft and unconstructed, this "knitting bag" version of the clutch bag is made of neon blue UltraSuede with a reverse appliqué design, accented with topstitch detailing and wooden dowel handles. Make this bag in various sizes and fabrics for special occasions or everyday, either for yourself or for a special friend.

MATERIALS

- Two 10" × 20" (25.5 cm × 51 cm) pieces of UltraSuede in different colors
- 24" (61 cm) wooden dowel, ⅜" (1 cm) in diameter
- Wood stain

TOOLS

- Sewing machine
- Matching thread
- Hand-sewing needle
- Scissors
- Utility knife or small scissors
- Fabric-marking pen or pencil
- Fabric glue
- Fine-toothed handsaw
- Paintbrush and soft cotton rags

GETTING STARTED

- To create the handle cutouts, modify the Clutch Bag pattern according to the following steps: First, add the UltraSuede Clutch Bag Handle pattern to the front edge of the Clutch Bag Front/Back pattern. Then, fold the Front/Back pattern in half on the center bottom line, and trace the handle cutout onto what was the flap and cut along this line. This new Front/Back pattern is symmetrical, both front to back and left to right.
- Trace the Front/Back and Clutch Bag Gusset patterns onto the UltraSuede, marking placement and stitching locations.
- Cut one front and back and two gussets from both pieces of UltraSuede.
- Transfer the flower with the fabric-marking pen or pencil to the clutch bag front, and cut out the flower from the outside fabric only, using the utility knife or small scissors.

1 Topstitch the outside and the lining gusset pieces together along the top, ⅛" (0.3 cm) from the raw edges.

2 Glue or hand baste together the edges of the outside and lining UltraSuede front and back pieces. Hand stitch around the flower cutout and along the stem.

3 Glue or baste the gussets to the front and back, matching the center bottom and top gusset marks.

4 Topstitch around the entire bag, including the gusset seams, ⅛" (0.3 cm) from the raw edge.

5 To create a channel for the wooden dowel, fold the top edges of the handle cutout 1" (2.5 cm) to the wrong side, as marked on the pattern. Topstitch ⅛" (0.3 cm) from the raw edge.

6 Using the fine-toothed handsaw, cut the wooden dowel into two 12" (30.5 cm) pieces. Apply the stain to the two handles with the paintbrush, and remove it with the soft cotton rags to the desired color.

7 When the handles are dry, slide them through the channels.

tips

Play with color combinations and cutout designs to create bags with different looks. Use home-decorating stencils for cutout inspiration, and paint the dowels with acrylic paint to add character to the bag.

CHAPTER 4

making drawstring bags

The drawstring bag originated as a man's bag: It was small and attached to the belt. During the sixteenth and seventeenth centuries, the drawstring pouch became known as a "cutpurse" and was used to hold coins. Robin Hood and his Merry Men would hide in the woods, and when a gentleman rode by on his horse, they would swing from the trees and cut the purse off of the man's belt.

The drawstring bag really came into fashion in the 1980s. Featured in a variety of fabrics and sizes, this style of handbag became a staple accessory. Nowadays, companies like Coach and Fendi have incorporated this bag into their mainstay lines. The construction of the drawstring bag is quite simple, requiring only one piece of fabric for the outside and one piece for the lining. By creating a channel and slipping cording through it, you create the drawstring effect.

Which fabric is best? Choose from quilted cottons, canvas, vinyl, or tapestry. Add satin cording with tassels, rope, or ribbon as your closure, and then add beads, sequins, embroidery, or appliqué to enhance your creation.

drawstring evening bag

What better way to express pure elegance and classic fashion than with velvet and rhinestones? Treat yourself to this stylish drawstring evening bag, designed to reflect your personality. Whether you choose velvet, tapestry, silk, or satin, this little number will spark up your evenings. Rhinestones or crystals shimmer and sparkle, but it's your own originality that crowns this bag as a majestic silhouette.

MATERIALS

- 22" × 9" (56 cm × 23 cm) piece of fabric for outside
- 22" × 9" (56 cm × 23 cm) piece of lining fabric
- 22" × 9" (56 cm × 23 cm) piece of iron-on fusible interfacing
- 168 rhinestones or crystals
- Two 14" (35.5 cm) ¼" (0.3 cm) lengths of cording for drawstring
- 56" (142 cm) of ½" (1.3 cm) cording for handle

TOOLS

- Sewing machine
- Matching thread
- Hand-sewing needle
- Scissors
- Air- or water-soluble marking pen
- Iron
- Fabric glue
- Loop turner

GETTING STARTED

- Press the fabrics to remove any wrinkles.
- Press the iron-on fusible interfacing to the wrong side of the outside fabric.
- Trace the Drawstring Evening Bag Front/Back and Bottom patterns onto the outside fabric and the lining fabrics, marking the notches, handle placement, and slit marks with the air- or water-soluble marking pen.
- Transfer all rhinestone placement markings onto the outside front piece using the air- or water-soluble marking pen, but make sure the marks aren't too large or too dark.
- Cut out all pieces.

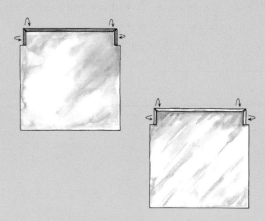

step 1 On the outside front and back, fold the top and side edges above the slit marks to the wrong side, then press if needed and glue in place. Clip the corners to reduce bulk. Repeat this step for the lining.

step 2 Glue the rhinestones or crystals onto the outside front at the markings.

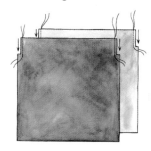

step 3 Topstitch the side edges along the ⅜" (1 cm) seam allowance in the channel areas only on the outside front and back. Repeat this step for the lining.

step 4 Cut the cording for the handle into two equal lengths. Make a small knot in all four ends of the cording to prevent the handle from slipping out of the seam. Hand tack the ends of the cording handle to the right side of the seam allowance on the front and back pieces at the handle placement markings.

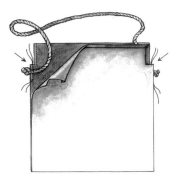

step 5 With right sides together, hand baste and machine sew the outside front and back at the side seams using ⅜" (1 cm) seam allowance. Be sure to catch the handle in the seam allowance. Repeat this step for the lining.

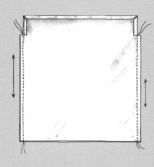

step 7 Sew a channel in the front and back by sewing two rows of parallel stitches through the outside and the lining, as indicated on the Front/Back pattern.

step 8 Starting on one side, use the loop turner to feed one length of the cording for the drawstring through the channel around the entire bag, coming out at the same side that you entered. Repeat this process for the other piece of cording, starting on the opposite side.

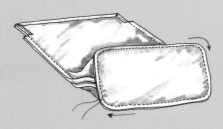

step 6 With right sides together, hand baste and machine sew the outside bottom to the outside front and back, matching the side seams and the notches at the center front and center. Repeat this step for the lining.

step 10 Tie knots in the ends of both drawstrings. Pull the drawstrings outward to close your evening bag.

tips > You can make this bag using any fabric, so get creative: Use dressier fabrics for a dressier bag, or everyday fabrics—such as burlap, cotton, or linen trimmed with fringe or tassels—for a more casual bag. Tired of rhinestones and crystals? For a club feel, use studs or eyelets on leather or suede; for a more exotic feel, try tapestry prints embellished with embroidery stitching.

step 9 Turn the outside bag right side out, and drop the lining into it so the wrong sides are together. Hand baste and machine topstitch the outside to the lining along the top edge, beginning above the channel area on one side, around both corners, and stopping at the channel area on the other side. Repeat this step for the front and back.

patchwork drawstring

If old-fashioned patchwork quilts make your heart flutter, our patchwork drawstring has it all. Made from pre-sewn patchwork cotton in red, white, and blue and trimmed with self-handle and silver grommets, this bag shows your support for your nation. For security and fun, the handle is attached with dog leash hooks.

MATERIALS

- ½ yard (46 cm) of outside fabric
- ½ yard (46 cm) of lining fabric
- 10 large silver grommets
- 2 dog leash or key ring hooks

TOOLS

- Sewing machine
- Matching thread
- Scissors
- Water-soluble marking pen
- Iron
- Large grommet-setting kit

GETTING STARTED

- Press the fabrics to remove any wrinkles.
- Enlarge the Drawstring Evening Bag patterns to 115%, and then trace the Front/Back and Bottom patterns onto the outside and lining fabrics, marking the notches, handle locations, and slit marks with the water-soluble marking pen.
- Mark the drawstring grommet locations 2" (5 cm) down from the top edge, centered 2" (5 cm) apart on the outside front and back.
- Cut out all pieces.
- Cut two 18" X 2¾" (45.5 X 7 cm) strips of outside fabric for the shoulder strap, one 30" X 1" (76 cm X 2.5 cm) strip of outside fabric for the drawstring, and a piece of 1¾" X 2½" (4.5 cm X 6.5 cm) fabric for the drawstring stopper.

1   With right sides together, sew the outside front and back pieces together along the side seams, using ⅜" (1 cm) seam allowance.

2   Hand baste and machine sew the outside bottom to the front and back with the right sides together. (Just be sure to match the bottom notches with the side seams and the center front and center back.)

3   Repeat Steps 1 and 2 for the lining.

4   Place the lining inside the outside bag with the right sides together. Sew the outside and the lining together around the top edge, using ⅜" (1 cm) seam allowance, leaving a 6" (15 cm) opening to turn the bag right side out.

5   Turn the bag right side out and topstitch around the top edge, ⅛" (0.3 cm) from the edge.

6   Sew the two 18" (46 cm) strap strips together along the short ends to form a 36" × 2¾" (91.5 cm × 7 cm) strap.

7   Fold the long edges of the strap ⅜" (1 cm) to the wrong side, and press. Fold the strap in half again, creating a 1" (2.5 cm) wide strap, and press. Topstitch ⅛" (0.3 cm) from both long edges. Hand or machine sew the strap ends to the key ring or dog leash hooks.

8   Repeat Step 6 with the 30" (76 cm) drawstring strip, folding the long edges of the strip ¼" (0.6 cm) to the wrong side and pressing. Then, fold the strip in half along the long edges so that it's ¼" (0.6 cm) wide, and press. Stitch down the center of the drawstring.

9   To create a 1" (2.5 cm) wide stopper for the drawstring, fold the long sides of the drawstring stopper down ⅜" (1 cm), and topstitch ⅛" (0.3 cm) from the turned edge. Sew the short ends together using ¼" (0.6 cm) seam allowance with the right sides together. Turn the stopper right side out, and stitch down the center to create two channels for the drawstring to go through.

10 Punch the grommet holes in the marked locations. Using the grommet-setting kit and following the manufacturer's instructions, set the grommets for the drawstring. Punch the grommet holes, and set one grommet at each side seam for the handles. Make sure the grommet is set the correct distance from the edge to accommodate the diameter of the key ring or dog leash hook.

11 Thread the drawstring through the grommets, slide the stopper on, and tie the ends of the drawstring together. Then, hook the key ring or dog leash hooks through the grommets.

tips

This bag can be fun, elegant, or sporty, depending on the fabric you use. You can even try creating your own patchwork pattern with your favorite fabrics. You can also make multiple straps to convert the bag from a shoulder bag to a handbag, or make the bottom firmer by gluing a piece of foam or cardboard to the bottom between the outside fabric and the lining.

drawstring backpack

This innovative interpretation of the classic drawstring bag gets its uniqueness and pizzazz from your choice of fabrics and embellishments. Whether it's ethnic and folksy or contemporary and modern, bold colors or sophisticated elegance, this simple bag really makes a statement.

MATERIALS

- ¼ yard (23 cm) of four different outside fabrics
- ½ yard (46 cm) of lining fabric
- 3 yards (274.5 cm) of ½" (1.3 cm) braided trim
- 5" × 10½" (12.5 cm × 27 cm) piece of Pellon

TOOLS

- Sewing machine
- Matching thread
- Hand-sewing needle
- Scissors
- Water-soluble marking pen
- Iron
- Loop turner

GETTING STARTED

- To create the panel sections of the backpack, modify the Drawstring Evening Bag pattern according to the following steps: First, enlarge the Drawstring Evening Bag Front/Back and Bottom pieces to 150%. (You can disregard the "channel" and "slit" markings.) Then, measure and mark 6¼" (16 cm) in from the top left corner and 6¼" (16 cm) in from the bottom left corner on the Front/Back pattern, and draw a vertical line connecting the two marks. Cut along the marked line, creating a 6¼" × 12" (16 cm × 30.5 cm) Front/Back pattern with ⅜" (1 cm) seam allowance around all edges. Mark a line 1" (2.5 cm) down from the top edge of the Front/Back pattern; this line will be the cutting line for the lining panels.
- Press the fabrics to remove any wrinkles.
- Trace the Front/Back pattern onto the outside and lining fabrics, marking the notches on the bottom pattern. (Be sure to cut the lining panels 1" [2.5 cm] shorter than the outside panels.)
- Trace the Bottom pattern onto the Pellon, the outside fabric, and the lining fabric.
- Cut out all pieces.

1   Sew the two front panels together using ⅜" (1 cm) seam allowance. Repeat this step for the back panels.

2   Sew the outside front and back panels together at the side seams using ⅜" (1 cm) seam allowance, leaving a ¾" (2 cm) opening 1⅜" (3.5 cm) from the top edges at both side seams to allow for insertion of the drawstring. Press the seams open with the iron.

3   Sew the outside bottom to the Pellon within the seam allowance. Cut two pieces of the braided trim 3½" (9 cm) long. Fold the braided trim in half, and sew the two loops within the seam allowance to the bottom 3" (7.5 cm) to the left and right of the center back notch.

4   Sew the outside bottom to the assembled outside bag using ⅜" (1 cm) seam allowance, matching the seams to the notches on the bottom.

5   Sew the lining front and back panels together at the side seams using ⅜" (1 cm) seam allowance. Press the seams open with the iron.

6   Sew the lining bottom to the assembled lining front and back panels, matching the seams to the bottom notches. Leave one-quarter open for turning the right side out in Step 7.

7   Drop the lining into the outside with the right sides together. Sew the outside and lining together around the top edge using ⅜" (1 cm) seam allowance.

8   Turn the bag right side out so that 1" (2.5) of the outside fabric is turned to the inside of the bag. Topstitch around the top, through the outside and the lining, 1" (2.5) from the edge. Hand stitch the bottom of the lining closed.

9   Starting on one side, use the loop turner to feed 1½ yards (137 cm) of the braided trim through the channel around the entire bag, coming out at the same side that you entered. Repeat this step with another 1½ yard (137 cm) piece of braided trim, starting on the opposite side.

10 Put the end of the braided trim coming from the left side through the bottom loop on the left, and sew the ends of the braided trim together. Repeat this step for the right side. Pull the sewn ends into the channel to hide them.

tips

To create a unique look, experiment with a combination of fabrics, or use one fabric and add a fringe trim in the seams between the panels. You can also exclude the bottom loops to make this bag a shoulder bag, or you can make it convertible for more versatility!

bamboo handle bucket bag

A more contemporary version of the old knitting bag, this handbag offers you the flexibility of a tote with its oversized bamboo handles. If you don't like bamboo, then try metal rings, embroidery hoops, or plastic bracelets. This bag can be fun, funky, or elegant just by changing the handles and the trim—so let your imagination go wild!

MATERIALS

- ½ yard (46 cm) of fabric for outside
- ½ yard (46 cm) of lining fabric
- ½ yard (46 cm) of iron-on fusible interfacing
- 70" (178 cm) of 1" (2.5 cm) wide braided trim
- 2 bamboo (or other type) rings for handles

TOOLS

- Sewing machine
- Matching thread
- Hand-sewing needle
- Scissors
- Fabric-marking pen or pencil
- Iron
- Craft glue
- Double-sided craft tape

GETTING STARTED

- Press the fabrics to remove any wrinkles.
- Press the iron-on fusible interfacing to the wrong side of the outside fabric.
- Enlarge the Drawstring Evening Bag patterns to 150%, and then trace them onto the outside fabric and lining fabric, marking the notches with the fabric-marking pen or pencil. (You can disregard the "channel" and "slit" markings.)
- Cut out all pieces.

1. Fold the top edges of the outside and lining fronts and backs ⅜" (1 cm) to the wrong side, press, and glue in place.

2. Place two strips of double-sided craft tape on the outside front and back where you want braided trim to go. Keep the ends of trim even with the raw edge of the bottom of the bag. Let the excess extend past the top edge for attaching the handles later.

3. Sew the trim to the outside fabric around all edges, but leave at least 1" (2.5 cm) free at the top edge, because that will later be sewn to the lining.

4. Place the outside front and back right sides together. Hand baste then machine sew the sides from the top to the bottom using ⅜" (1 cm) seam allowance.

5. Repeat Step 4 for the lining.

6. With right sides together, hand baste and machine sew the outside bottom to the outside front and back, matching the side seams and the notches at the center front and center back.

7. Repeat Step 6 to attach the lining bottom to the lining front and back.

8. Turn the outside bag right side out. Loop the extra trim over the bamboo rings, and temporarily attach the trim to inside of bag using the double-sided adhesive tape.

9. Drop the lining into the outside bag. Hand baste and machine topstitch ⅛" (0.3 cm) from the top edge, being sure to catch the trim between both layers.

rainy-day shoulder bag

Fashion doesn't have to take a back seat when the weather is nasty. In fact, that's the time to bring out your brightest and cheeriest accessories. Put Mother Nature in her place with this rainy-day shoulder bag. Using water-resistant fabrics and nylon webbing, you can create a shoulder bag that will have even the most puddle-conscious heads turning. Then, feel free to add your own personalized touches: add trims and embellishments, change the color of the flap, add a cell phone holder or beeper keeper—and make those rain clouds disappear!

MATERIALS

- 1 yard (91.5 cm) of water-resistant fabric for outside and lining
- 2 yards (183 cm) of 2" (5 cm) wide webbing
- ½ yard (46 cm) of 1" (2.5 cm) wide trim
- 1¼ yards (114.5 cm) of 1" (2.5 cm) binding or ribbon
- One 2" (5 cm) plastic strap loop
- One 2" (5 cm) plastic strap single bar slide
- One 1" (2.5 cm) side-release buckle

TOOLS

- Sewing machine
- Matching thread
- Scissors
- Water-soluble marking pen
- Double-sided craft tape

GETTING STARTED

- Enlarge the Drawstring Evening Bag patterns to 150%, then trace two Drawstring Evening Bag Front/Back and Bottom, and one Shoulder Bag Flap pattern onto the fabric.
- Mark all locations on the flap for the stripe, buckle, and strap. (You can disregard the "channel" and "slit" markings on the Front/Back pattern.)
- Cut out all pieces.

1   Tape down the 2" (5 cm) trim with double-sides craft tape. Topstitch the 2" (5 cm) trim down the center of the outside front, back, and outside flap, ⅛" (0.3 cm) from the long edges.

2   Cut a 6" (15 cm) piece of the 2" (5 cm) wide webbing, and thread the plastic strap loop onto it. Fold the webbing in half, and machine sew the ends within the seam allowance onto the back edge of the outside flap, as marked on the Shoulder Bag Flap pattern. Use 50" (127 cm) of the 2" (5 cm) webbing for the strap. Sew one end of the strap to the back edge of the flap within the seam allowance in the placement location.

3   With right sides together, sew the outside flap to the outside back matching the centers and using ⅜" (1 cm) seam allowance. (The flap is smaller than the back by ⅜" [1 cm] on each side.) Topstitch the seam allowance down ⅛" (0.3 cm) from the seam.

4   With right sides together, sew the outside front and back side seams together using ⅜" (1 cm) seam allowance.

5   Cut a 10" (25.5 cm) piece of the 1" (2.5 cm) wide webbing, and sew it within the seam allowance to the center bottom of the outside front. Sew the outside bottom to the outside front and back, using ⅜" (1 cm) seam allowance.

6   Cut a 6" (15 cm) piece of the 1" (2.5 cm) wide webbing, and thread the "female" part of the side-release buckle onto it. Box stitch the loop onto the lining flap so that the raw ends are folded under the box stitch, as marked on the Shoulder Bag Flap pattern.

7   Sew the lining flap to the lining back with the right sides together, using ⅜" (1 cm) seam allowance. (The flap is smaller than the back by ⅜" [1 cm] on each side.)

8   Sew the lining bottom to the lining front and back with the right sides together, using ⅜" (1 cm) seam allowance.

9   Place the lining inside the outside of the bag with the right sides together, and sew around the front top edge using ⅜" (1 cm) seam allowance.

10   Turn the bag right side out, and topstitch around the front ⅛" (0.3 cm) from the top edge.

11   With wrong sides together, sew the outside lining flaps together ⅛" (0.3 cm) from the raw edges. Fold the 1" (2.5 cm) wide binding or ribbon over the raw edges of the flap, and topstitch ¼" (0.6 cm) from the edge. (*Note:* Iron the binding or ribbon in half first for a neater finish.)

12   Thread the "male" section of the side-release buckle onto the 1" (2.5 cm) wide webbing on the outside front. Fold over the end of the webbing, and stitch it down to secure the buckle. Place the strap through the 2" (5 cm) single bar slide and through the loop, and then sew the end back onto the single bar slide.

tips

For an added touch, make a cell-phone pocket to match your bag, and attach it to the strap. To add more color, cut the outside flap from a different fabric.

CHAPTER 5

making beach bags

Have you ever wished that your beach bag was three times its size, or that it had pockets and a place to put your water bottle, suntan lotion, cell phone, and Walkman? Well, your prayers have been answered. Designed originally as a classic tote bag, the beach bag has evolved into a highly organized, compartmentalized, and specialized bag.

Beach bags became popular in the 1960s. They were used to tote sun-and-sand paraphernalia back and forth from the car to the beach or pool. Used also for short trips, the beach bag has become a mainstay in everyone's wardrobe. This bag isn't just for women: Men find it a great carryall for camping, boating, or stashing emergency equipment in the car.

Using one fabric for the body of the bag, another for the pockets, and a third for the lining, you can create a personalized bag to suit your needs. By lengthening or shortening the handles, you can carry this bag on your shoulder or in your hand. Consider using canvas, terry cloth, vinyl, or quilted cotton. Use an iron-on transfer to make your bag easily identifiable, or embellish it with decorative webbing, appliqué, or embroidered patches.

beach bag

A day at the beach or by the pool can be a fun-filled experience or a disaster, depending on how your supplies get there. This season, travel in style and confidence with our fully organized beach bag tote. Vinyl pockets on the outside allow you to keep your suntan lotion, water, sunglasses, and keys right where you want them. And the sky's the limit when it comes to the size and number of pockets you can add to this bag. Make a beach bag for a friend—it's a great gift!

MATERIALS

- 21" × 30" (53.5 cm × 76 cm) piece of terry cloth
- 21" × 22" (53.5 cm × 56 cm) piece of clear vinyl
- 21" × 30" (53.5 cm × 76 cm) piece of lining fabric
- 104" (264 cm) length of 1" (2.5 cm) wide webbing
- 42" (106.5 cm) length of 1" (2.5 cm) wide grosgrain ribbon

TOOLS

- Sewing machine
- Matching thread
- Pins
- Scissors
- Water-soluble marking pen
- Iron

GETTING STARTED

- Press the terry cloth and lining fabric to remove any wrinkles.
- Enlarge and trace the Beach Bag Front/Back and Pocket patterns onto the terry cloth and clear vinyl, following the instructions on the pattern pieces.
- Transfer all placement locations for the pockets and handles onto the terry cloth with the water-soluble marking pen, and then transfer the topstitching lines onto the vinyl with the water-soluble marking pen.
- Cut two 52" (132 cm) lengths of 1" (2.5 cm)–wide webbing.
- Cut two 21" (53.5 cm) lengths of 1" (2.5 cm)–wide grosgrain.

step 1 On a setting appropriate for grosgrain ribbon, press the 1" (2.5 cm) wide ribbon in half, matching the long edges to create the ½" (1.3 cm) binding for the vinyl pockets. Fold the ribbon over the top edge of the vinyl pockets, and topstitch through all three layers, ⅜" (1 cm) from the folded edge.

step 2 Matching the raw edges, lay the vinyl pockets onto the terry cloth front and back pieces, and stitch them in place within the ⅜" (1 cm) seam allowance. (This stitching will be hidden when the front and back pieces are joined.)

step 3 Pin one short end of one 52" (132 cm) length of the 1" (2.5) wide webbing to the right bottom of the beach bag front, matching the raw edges. Continue to pin the webbing to the front, following the markings transferred from the Beach Bag Front/Back pattern. Topstitch the 1" (2.5 cm) webbing ⅛" (0.3 cm) from the long edges onto the front. Box stitch the webbing at the top to add durability. Repeat this step to attach the other end of the same piece of webbing to the left bottom of the beach bag front, making sure the webbing remains flat and untwisted. Repeat this step with the other 52" (132 cm) length of webbing on the beach bag back. (*Note*: The handles should go from front to front and back to back.)

step 4 To define the sides and bottom of the pockets, topstitch along the lines marked on the terry cloth.

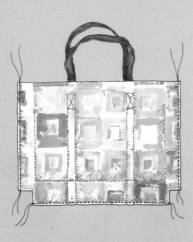

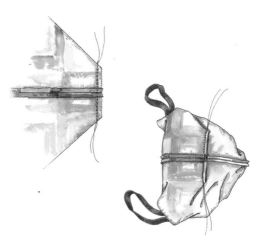

step 5 With right sides together, sew the beach bag front to the back, stitching down the side seams and across the bottom using ⅜" (1 cm) seam allowance. Just be careful not to catch the handles in the seams.

step 6 To create the flat bottom, pull the bottom and side seams open. With right sides together, match the side and bottom seams, and then stitch straight across the opening using ⅜" (1 cm) seam allowance. The bottom seam will be perpendicular to the side seams. Repeat Steps 5 and 6 for the lining.

tips > Using a beach towel is a fun alternative for the outside fabric. Try your hand at customizing the sizes of the pockets for all your beach supplies by sewing the vinyl pieces on after the webbing is attached. You can also add pockets to the lining.

step 7 Tuck the handles into the terry-cloth bag, place the lining inside so the right sides of both fabrics are together and the top raw edges are even, and pin the layers together. Stitch around the top of the bag using ⅜" (1 cm) seam allowance, but be sure to leave a 6" (15 cm) opening through which you can turn the bag right side out.

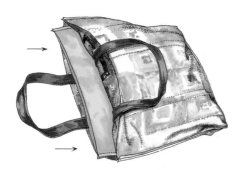

step 8 Turn the bag right side out, and fold the seam allowances of the opening to the wrong side and press. Topstitch at ¼" (0.6 cm) around the top edge, making sure the opening is stitched closed.

vintage necktie oversized tote bag

Have you ever noticed those old ties hanging in the back of your husband's closet, waiting for fashion to repeat itself? Don't even think about throwing them out! Instead, use them to create this one-of-a-kind tribute to his old ties. This vintage bag incorporates those wide out-of-fashion ties as handles and pockets. After your friends see you with it, they'll be begging for one of their own.

MATERIALS

- 1 yard (91.5 cm) of fabric for outside
- 1 yard (91.5 cm) of lining fabric
- 1 yard (91.5 cm) of quilt batting or felt
- 6 vintage neckties
- 15" × 4" (38 cm × 10 cm) piece of lightweight cardboard (optional)

TOOLS

- Sewing machine
- Matching thread
- Hand-sewing needle
- Scissors
- Fabric-marking pen or pencil
- Iron
- Craft glue
- Double-sided craft tape

GETTING STARTED

- Press the fabrics and neckties to remove any wrinkles.
- Enlarge and trace the Vintage Necktie Oversized Tote Bag Front/Back pattern onto the outside fabric and lining fabric, following the instructions on the pattern pieces.
- Using the fabric-marking pen or pencil, mark the tie corner and tie handle placement lines on the front, and then flip the pattern and mark the placement lines on the back. (That way, the thinner and wider parts of the tie handles will line up when bag is sewn together.)
- Cut out all pieces.
- When cutting out the felt or quilt batting, be sure to eliminate the ⅜" (1 cm) turn-in allowance on the top edges.

1 Lightly glue the felt or quilt batting to the wrong side of the outside front and back of the bag, placing the raw edge of the felt or batting ⅜" (1 cm) below the raw edge of the fabric. Fold the top edge of the front and back ⅜" (1 cm) to the wrong side, and glue it onto the felt or batting. Fold the top edge of the lining fabric ⅜" (1 cm) to the wrong side, and glue it in place.

2 Using the double-sided craft tape, place the tie handles and the tie "corners" onto the outside front, following the placement markings. When cutting off the corners of the ties, leave some extra fabric on the raw edges. Once they're taped down to the fabric, topstitch ⅛" (0.3 cm) from all of the edges, including the corner of the tote bag. Then topstitch ⅛" (0.3 cm) around each necktie handle, stopping at the top of the bag. Repeat this step to attach the tie corners and the ends of the tie handles to the back of the bag, being careful not to twist the ties.

3 To make the tie pockets for the inside lining, cut the next 6½" (16.5 cm) of three of the ties that were cut for the corners; these will be the pockets. Then cut 13" (33 cm) off the narrow end of the remaining tie, and fold and glue down both ends of the raw edges. This will bind the top edge of the pockets. Next, using the double-sided tape, insert the top raw edges of the three cut "pockets" into the inside center of the narrow tie piece, lining them up side by side. Fold the 13" (33 cm) narrow piece in half, and topstitch across, catching the ties inside. Then, fold and tape down the bottom cut edges of the "pockets" so that the raw edges are on the inside, and place them right side down on the front or back of the lining where you want them to go. Then topstitch ⅛" (0.3 cm) across the bottom and down both sides of each "tie pocket" (six sides total) onto lining, leaving the tops open.

4 Place the outside front and back right sides together, making sure not to catch the tie handles in the side seam allowances. Hand baste and then machine stitch along sides from the top to bottom, then across the bottom, using ⅜" (1 cm) seam allowance and leaving the bottom corners open. To create the flat bottom, pull the bottom and side seams open. With right sides together, match the side and bottom seams, and then stitch straight across the opening using ⅜" (1 cm) seam allowance. The bottom seam will be perpendicular to the side seams.

5 Repeat Step 4 for the lining.

6 Press the side seams of the outside bag open, and turn it right side out. For extra durability, you can lightly glue the piece of lightweight cardboard to the inside bottom of the bag, but first press open the inside bottom seams.

7 Press the side seams of the lining open, and drop the lining into the outside bag. Match the top edges, and use the double-sided craft tape to hold the two layers together.

8 Topstitch ⅛" (0.3 cm) around the top edge of the bag.

flower-printed carryall

Perk up your spring and summer accessories collection with flower power. This floral printed cotton carryall is perfect for shopping, lunching with friends, or just relaxing by the pool. Lined in a solid color with coordinated straps, this bag is an ideal accessory. Use antique buttons or vintage fabrics as an alternative to the floral print, or create a mother-daughter collection by using a smaller-sized pattern.

MATERIALS

- 1 yard (91.5 cm) of printed fabric
- 1 yard (91.5 cm) of solid colored fabric
- 2 yards (183 cm) of 1" (2.5 cm) wide webbing
- 1 button
- 6" (15 cm) length of rattail

TOOLS

- Sewing machine
- Matching thread
- Pins
- Hand-sewing needle
- Scissors
- Water-soluble marking pen
- Iron

GETTING STARTED

- Press the fabric to remove any wrinkles.
- Enlarge the Beach Bag Front/Back pattern to 150%, then trace two Front/Back pattern pieces onto the printed fabric, marking the handle location with the water-soluble marking pen or pencil.
- Trace two Front/Back pattern pieces onto the lining.
- Cut out all pieces.
- Reduce the pocket pattern to create the two outside accent pieces by measuring and cutting 4½" (11.5 cm) from the top edge of the pattern. Trace and cut two of these pieces from the solid-colored fabric.
- Cut two 36" × 1¾" (91.5 cm × 4.5 cm) pieces of the solid-colored fabric for the handles.
- Cut the 1" (2.5 cm) webbing into two 36" (91.5 cm) lengths.

1   Fold the long edges of the solid-colored handle pieces ⅜" (1 cm) to the wrong side to create two 1" × 36" (2.5 cm × 91.5 cm) pieces.

2   Topstitch the solid-colored handle pieces onto the 1" (2.5 cm) webbing, stitching ⅛" (0.3 cm) from the long edges.

3   Pin one short end of one handle to the right bottom of the bag front, matching the raw edges. Continue to pin the handle to the front, following the markings transferred from the Beach Bag Front/Back pattern. Topstitch the webbing ⅛" (0.3 cm) from the long edges onto the front. Box stitch the webbing at the top to strengthen the handle. Repeat this step to attach the opposite end of the same piece of webbing to the left side of the beach bag front, making sure that the webbing remains flat and untwisted. Repeat this step for the second handle on the back of the bag. (*Note*: The handles should go from front to front and back to back.)

4   Fold the top edges of the solid-colored accent pieces ⅜" (1 cm) to the wrong side and press.

5   Pin the solid-colored accent pieces to the front and back of the bag, matching the raw edges. Topstitch the accent pieces in place ⅛" (0.3 cm) from the finished edges.

6   With right sides together, sew the front and back pieces together at the side seams and across the bottom using ⅜" (1 cm) seam allowance, making sure you don't catch the handles in the seams.

7   To create the flat bottom, pull the bottom and side seams open. With right sides together, match the side and bottom seams, and then stitch straight across the opening using ⅜" (1 cm) seam allowance. (The bottom seam will be perpendicular to the side seams.)

8   Repeat Steps 6 and 7 for the lining.

9   Hand stitch the button to the center front of the bag 1⅜" (3.5 cm) from the top edge. Fold the 6" (15 cm) piece of rattail in half, forming a loop, and tack the ends to the top edge of the center back within the seam allowance.

10   Drop the lining into the outside of the bag so that the right sides of both fabrics are together. Pin and stitch around the top raw edges using the ⅜" (1 cm) seam allowance and leaving a 6" (15 cm) opening to turn the bag right side out. (*Note*: Make sure the handles are tucked inside between the outside and lining.)

11   Turn the bag right side out. Topstitch ⅛" (0.3 cm) around the top edge, making sure the opening from Step 10 is stitched closed.

tips

Use a remnant of the printed fabric to create a pocket or two inside the lining. Embroider your initials on the front of the bag by hand or by machine. Or, select another fastener as a closure—such as a snap, a tie, a hook-and-loop fastener, or a button and buttonhole.

silk scarf tote

What can you do with your collection of scarves when you've grown tired of them? Keep your favorites and turn them into new accessories. Made from one large scarf or shawl, this tote bag will turn heads and make your friends envious.

MATERIALS

- 1 large scarf with a border design
  (about 35" [89 cm] square)
- 1 yard (91.5 cm) of lining fabric
- 1 yard (91.5 cm) of felt or quilt batting
- 1 yard (91.5 cm) of fusible interfacing
- 1 small magnetic snap (½" [1.3 cm] diameter)
  with washers

TOOLS

- Sewing machine
- Matching thread
- Hand-sewing needle
- Scissors
- Fabric-marking pen or pencil
- Iron
- Utility or craft knife
- Craft glue
- Double-sided craft tape

GETTING STARTED

- Press the scarf and the lining fabric to remove any wrinkles.
- Enlarge and trace the Silk Scarf Tote Front/Back patterns onto the felt, fusible interfacing, and lining fabric, following the instructions on the pattern pieces, and then transfering all the markings with the fabric-marking pen or pencil.
- Cut out all pieces except for the outside scarf pieces. When cutting out the felt or quilt batting, be sure to eliminate the ⅜" (1 cm) turn-in allowance on the top edges.
- Place the front and back fusible interfacing pieces on the wrong side of the desired area of the scarf, and press them in place.
- Cut out the scarf front and back pieces around edges of the interfacing.

1 Lightly glue the felt or batting to the wrong sides of the bag front and back, placing the top edge of the felt or batting ⅜" (1 cm) below the raw edge of the scarf fabric. Fold the top edge of the scarf fabric ⅜" (1 cm) to the wrong side, and glue it to the felt or batting.

2 To make the flap, trace and cut a solid piece of fabric from the scarf center. Or, if needed, seam together the smaller leftover corner pieces of the scarf to get the finished size of the flap. Trace the Silk Scarf Tote Flap pattern onto the interfacing and the lining, following the instructions on the pattern. Press the interfacing to the back of the lining and the scarf fabric, and then fold the edges ⅜" (1 cm) to the wrong side and glue them to the interfacing. Clip any excess fabric from the corners as needed. Following the markings on the Flap pattern, cut slits in the lining flap with the utility or craft knife, and insert the "male" half of the magnetic snap, following the manufacturer's instructions. With wrong sides together, use the double-sided craft tape to attach the edges of the lining to the scarf fabric. Topstitch around the flap ⅛" (0.3 cm) from the edge.

3 Topstitch the back of the flap onto the back piece, following the placement and stitching lines on the Flap and Front/Back patterns. Cut slits in the front of the bag, and attach the "female" half of the magnetic snap, following the manufacturer's instructions.

4 Place the outside front and back right sides together. Hand baste and then machine stitch along the sides and the bottom, using ⅜" (1 cm) seam allowance and leaving the corners open. To create the flat bottom, pull the bottom and side seams open. With right sides together, match the side and bottom seams, and then stitch straight across the opening using ⅜" (1 cm) seam allowance. (The bottom seam will be perpendicular to the side seams.) Turn the bag right side out, and press the side seams open.

5 Repeat Step 4 for the lining.

6 To make the handle, cut across the larger leftover scarf corners (see diagram below), and hand baste a running stitch along the longer cut sides of both pieces. Gather the basted sides until they measure 6" (15 cm). Apply the double-sided craft tape along the gathered edges. Turn the outside bag right side out, and tuck one handle inside the bag at the top edge of each side seam.

7 Press the side seams of the lining open, and drop the lining into the bag so that the wrong sides of the fabric are together. Match the top raw edges, and use the double-sided craft tape to hold the edges in place.

8 Topstitch ⅛" (0.3 cm) around the top edge of the bag. Tie the ends of the handles together.

tips

If you don't want to use a magnetic snap, try a different closure, such as hook-and-loop fastener, sew-on snaps, a button, ribbon tie, or frogs.

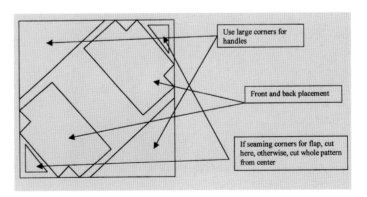

Use large corners for handles

Front and back placement

If seaming corners for flap, cut here, otherwise, cut whole pattern from center

GALLERY OF DESIGNS

Inspiration is defined as "a sudden brilliant idea"—and the Gallery of Designs is just that. It's like Alice in Wonderland's looking through that tiny keyhole and finding a world filled with wonderful creations.

All handbags in the Gallery were made using the basic master patterns, following the instructions for the master projects to the letter, and then adding unique trims, fabrics, and decorative stitching to create one-of-a-kind bags. Each serves as inspiration—to help you find your own sudden brilliant idea and visualize your own handbag wonderland. Your creativity and imagination await you!

Special thanks to the senior accessories design students for paving the creative road for you. They're truly an exceptional bunch of handbag designers.

TITLE: Rainforest Mist
STUDENT: Yi Jen Cheng
PATTERN: Clutch Bag

Any young lady would be pleased to carry this multicolored fabric clutch with an asymmetrical smocked flap. Perched on top of the flap is a handmade leather flower so real you have to resist smelling it. This bag is lined with raw silk. Instead of a snap, an apparel hook and eye closure was used.

TITLE: The Barbie Deluxe

STUDENT: Samantha Chère Beckerman

PATTERN: Tote Bag

If I were Barbie, I would definitely be carrying this bag. It's a showstopper! Made of shocking pink and red plaid wool and trimmed with fur, this tote bag definitely makes a trendy fashion statement. Barbie herself is appliquéd on the front to add just a pinch more drama.

TITLE: Shi Sheng
STUDENT: Cheryl Greenblatt
PATTERN: Clutch Bag

A touch of the Orient, a whisper of the Far East, this clutch bag with V-shaped flap is made of upholstery fabric. The bag becomes convertible simply by using a frog closure and adding a handle. The red tassels on each side of the bag makes this accessory statement fit for an empress.

TITLE: "Par Four" Tote
STUDENT: Cheryl Greenblatt
PATTERN: Tote Bag

Argyle print isn't just for golf socks anymore. This lively tote sports an argyle print upholstery fabric both front and back, with floral tapestry upholstery fabric gusset and handles. Swarovski crystals sparkle on the front and back to give this bag just a hint of glamour and sophistication.

TITLE: USA All the Way
STUDENT: Linda Diane Polichetti
PATTERN: Tote Bag

God Bless America, land that I love... To show your true patriotic feelings, try your hand at this flag-waving, original tote bag. Made of screen-printed cotton with a clear vinyl overlay, this bag is sure to put a smile on anyone's face and inspire a sense of pride as big as these United States.

TITLE: Accessories under Glass Tote
STUDENT: Linda Diane Polichetti
PATTERN: Tote Bag

You can never have enough accessories, and there's no better way to show off those accessories than with a tote bag that incorporates your favorites. This unique tote is made of turquoise vinyl covered with a clear plastic overlay. The "accessories" hiding behind the clear plastic are trimmed with beads, feathers, and ribbons to complete the look. The bag is perfect for rainy-day errands or summer days at the beach or pool.

TITLE: Underwear Drawer Clutch
STUDENT: Jessica Todd
PATTERN: Clutch Bag

"Bold and daring" best describes this little bag. The cotton zebra print clutch with shocking pink gussets and pink ruffled trim would put anyone in a dancing mood. Want to samba? Velcro closure and fuchsia lining makes this bag the envy of all.

TITLE: "Doris the Groupie's" Tote
STUDENT: Kelley Herron
PATTERN: Beach Bag

There is just no limit to the amount of things you can put on a bag and still have it look great. Here's the proof. One side of this tote is a black vinyl pocket with a bandana print and pink ball fringe, and the other side is an orange jersey pocket with a cotton print, accented by a fuchsia flower. The handles are made of pom-poms in an assortment of color and sizes. You never have to feel over dressed or underdressed with this bag, simply change the side you carry, and you'll be the hit at any gathering.

TITLE: Trilse Clutch
STUDENT: Ines Kim
PATTERN: Clutch Bag

The short shoulder bag is the hot new accessory. Here's an opportunity to create your own. Made of embossed leather with red wool lining, satin cord closure, and red contrasting stitching, this bag exudes classic design.

TITLE: Marine Biology
STUDENT: Ines Kim
PATTERN: Beach Bag

This oversized denim tote, with center pocket and modified self-handles, adds an element of sophistication to a casual fabric. The tablecloth lining offers a bit of whimsy, and the topstitching adds detail highlights. This tote is perfect for work or play.

TITLE: Edwardian Clutch
STUDENT: Veronica Cajucom
PATTERN: Clutch Bag

If you're a person who gets excited about vintage detailing, this is the bag for you. This clutch bag sports black ruffle lace and stitched-down pleating on the flap. An impressive antique button nicely finishes off the bag. This clutch bag is just the right style for an evening on the town or dinner and a movie with friends.

TITLE: Red Riding Hood Revisited
STUDENT: Erendira Tristan
PATTERN: Beach Bag

Little Red Riding Hood would be deliciously pleased to be carrying this tote, made of red velvet to match her hood and accentuated by an embroidered pocket and black velvet handles. Contrasting blanket stitching around the pocket and top of the bag adds to its appeal. This bag is sure to turn every wolf's head.

TITLE: Generation Gap Drawstring
STUDENT: Cary Mitsi Nomiyama
PATTERN: Drawstring Bag

Worn out your jeans but just can't part with them? Well, turn them into this terrific drawstring bag, accentuated by self-fringe and a hand-beaded pocket. The strap is a leopard print and turquoise chiffon with gold and turquoise disc detailing. This bag is sure to be a hit, whether you're at the mall or on the town.

TITLE: All That Glitters
STUDENT: Cary Mitsi Nomiyama
PATTERN: Clutch Bag

Shimmer and shine with this iridescent blue mini clutch bag, with bronze bead appliqué frog closure. The hand-sewn, blanket-stitched edging and gold rings complete the silhouette.

TITLE: Pirate's Cove
STUDENT: Cary Mitsi Nomiyama
PATTERN: Clutch Bag

A little sophistication and a lot of pizzazz, this mini clutch has it all—from the herringbone wool body to the contrasting wool lining. Hand-trimmed with turquoise and silver bugle beads and gold-coin accent, this bag will make anyone feel special.

TITLE: Dory Tote
STUDENT: Jury Artola
PATTERN: Tote Bag

Classic and elegant, this boiled wool tote with reverse appliqué would make a perfect accessory for work or play. This tote will complement everything from a suit to a great pair of slacks. Start a trend: Make several in different sizes and carry more than one.

TITLE: Pinky's Pink Clutch
STUDENT: Celina Guity
PATTERN: Clutch Bag

Pretty in pink, this mini velvet clutch bag has a multicolored, interchangeable tie closure.
Slipped between three gold grommets, the tie allows the bag to expand or contract, depending
on what's inside.

TITLE: L'Automne Jardin Tote
STUDENT: Rika Maeda
PATTERN: Beach Bag

Whether you use this bag to carry your knitting or your personal items, this bamboo-handled tote is sure to make an impression. Made of green wool with striped cotton pocket, handmade wool flowers with accent beading, and embroidered detailing, this floral tote makes the perfect accessory for any occasion.

TITLE: Military Fantasy
STUDENT: Jaymie Stroud
PATTERN: Clutch Bag

Camouflage fabric, traditionally used for military clothing, finds a home in this stylish clutch bag. This bag is trimmed with feminine, white ruffled lace, accented with camouflage fringe. The lining features a denim-stripe fabric and hook-and-loop closure. For added detail, fabric paint squiggles cover the flap.

TITLE: Kit Royale
STUDENT: Katharine M. Wall
PATTERN: Beach Bag

Pure, simple, classic, and *elegant* are words that describe this tote. Made of purple and magenta boiled wool with a self-handle and accented with silver grommets, this tote will take you anywhere you want to go—in style.

TITLE: Colonial Denim Clutch
STUDENT: Keeva Halferty
PATTERN: Clutch Bag

It looks like a lingerie case, but it's really a small clutch made of indigo denim with complementary cotton-striped lining and a self-tie closure.

TITLE: Streets of Gold
STUDENT: Mokgadi Matlhako
PATTERN: Tote Bag

Graffiti isn't just for walls anymore. This rustic tote bag is made of raw-seamed leather, with an original screen that has been spray painted on the body of the bag. Raw leather handles are attached with rivets. This tote can be worn with jeans, military garb, or your favorite leather pants.

TITLE: All Stars Tote

STUDENT: Mokgadi Matlhako

PATTERN: Tote Bag

Here's a tote that can pay tribute to your favorite sport, team, or rock star: This bag immortalizes the players in the NBA. Made of clear vinyl laminate, with a montage of photos in between and attached with silver rivets, this stylized tote is a slam-dunk hit on any playing field.

master patterns

Tote Bag Front/Back

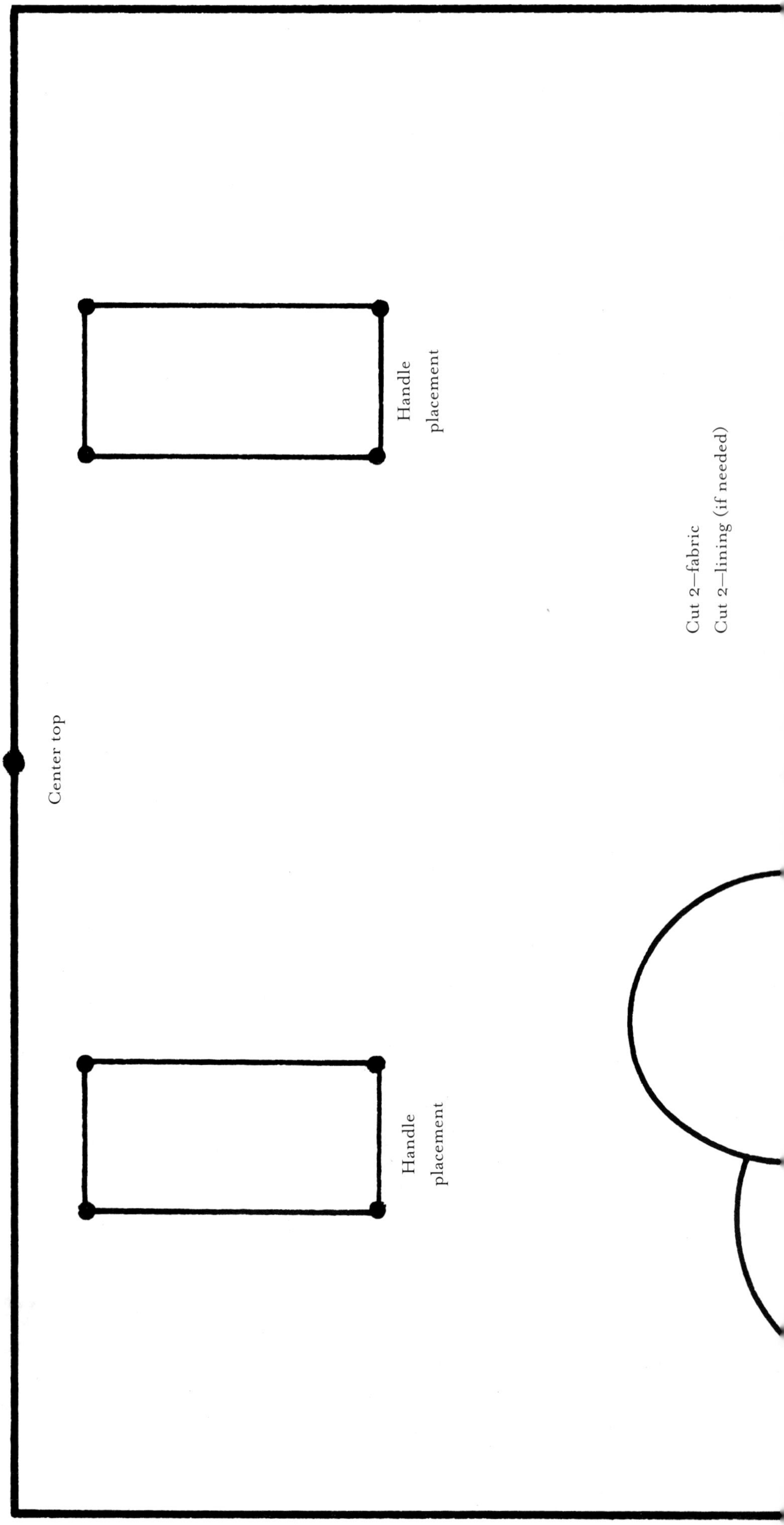

Handle placement

Handle placement

Center top

Cut 2—fabric

Cut 2—lining (if needed)

Beach Bag Front/Back

Photocopy at 200%

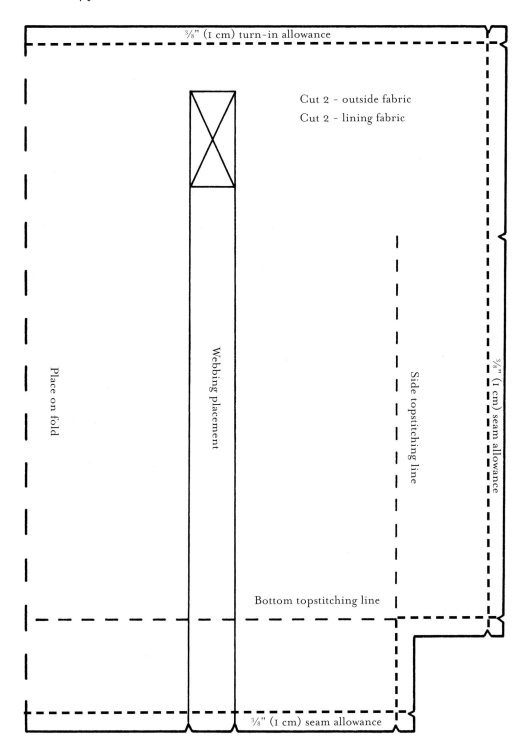

³⁄₈" (1 cm) turn-in allowance

Cut 2 - outside fabric

Cut 2 - lining fabric

Place on fold

Webbing placement

Side topstitching line

³⁄₈" (1 cm) seam allowance

Bottom topstitching line

³⁄₈" (1 cm) seam allowance

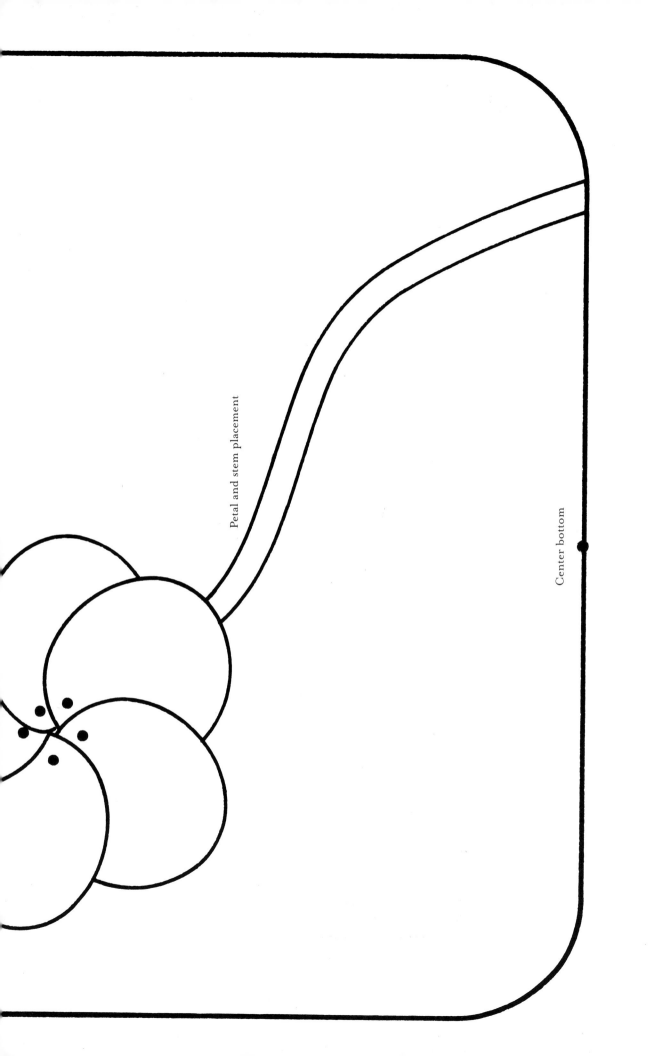

Petal and stem placement

Center bottom

Tote Bag Bottom/Gusset
Photocopy at 200%

Cut 2—fabric
Cut 2—lining (if needed)

Center bottom

⅜" (1 cm) seam allowance

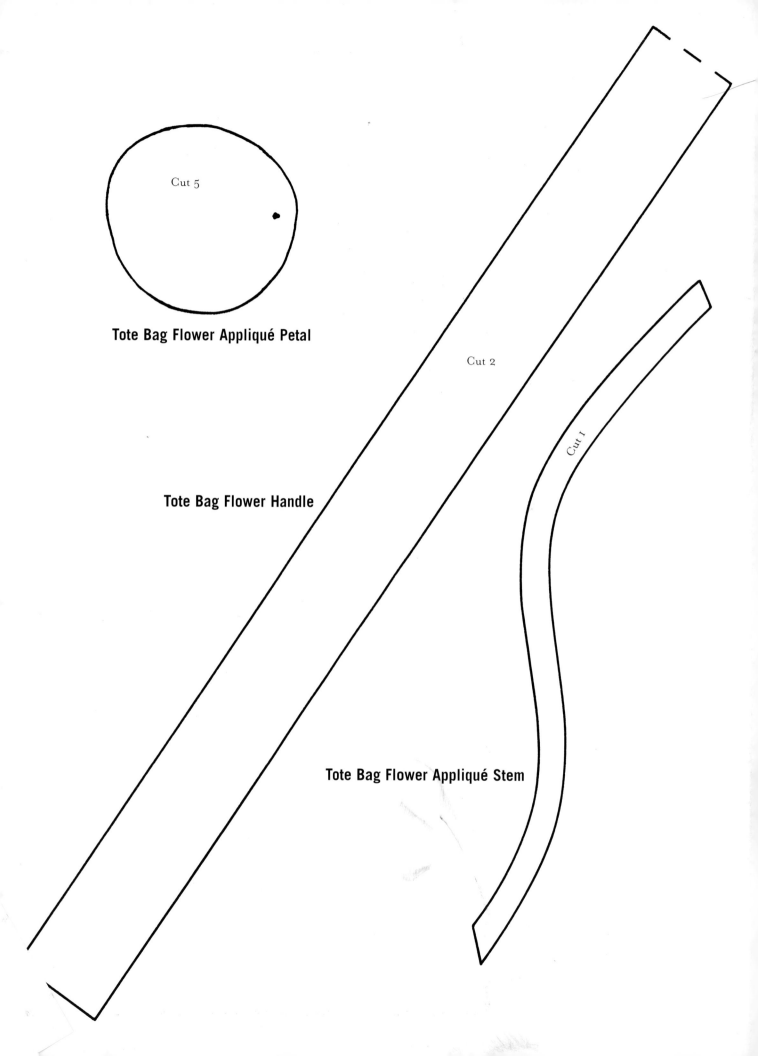

Cut 5

Tote Bag Flower Appliqué Petal

Cut 2

Cut 1

Tote Bag Flower Handle

Tote Bag Flower Appliqué Stem

Clutch Bag Gusset

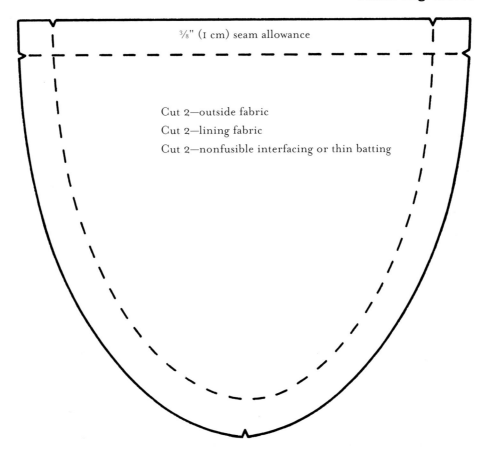

⅜" (1 cm) seam allowance

Cut 2—outside fabric
Cut 2—lining fabric
Cut 2—nonfusible interfacing or thin batting

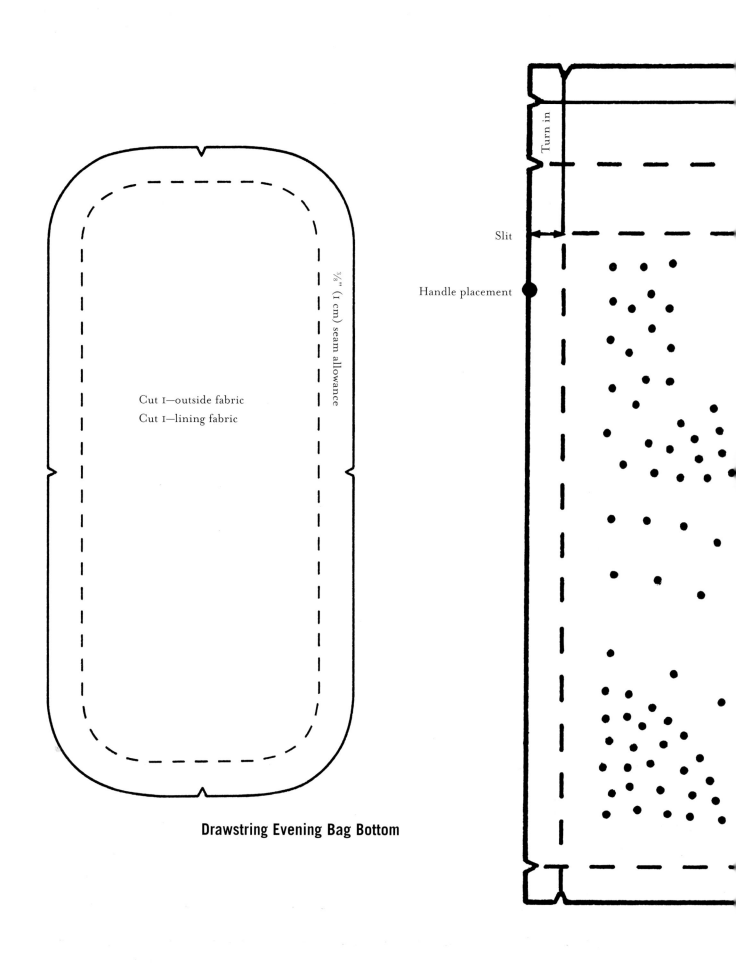

Cut I—outside fabric
Cut I—lining fabric

$\frac{3}{8}$" (I cm) seam allowance

Drawstring Evening Bag Bottom

Turn in

Slit

Handle placement

³⁄₈" (I cm) seam allowance

Cut I

Center bottom of gusset

Front

Transfer to front of outside fabric for closure placement

Top of gusset

For UltraSuede Clutch Bag, attach Handle Cutout pattern to this side.

Drawstring Evening Bag Front/Back

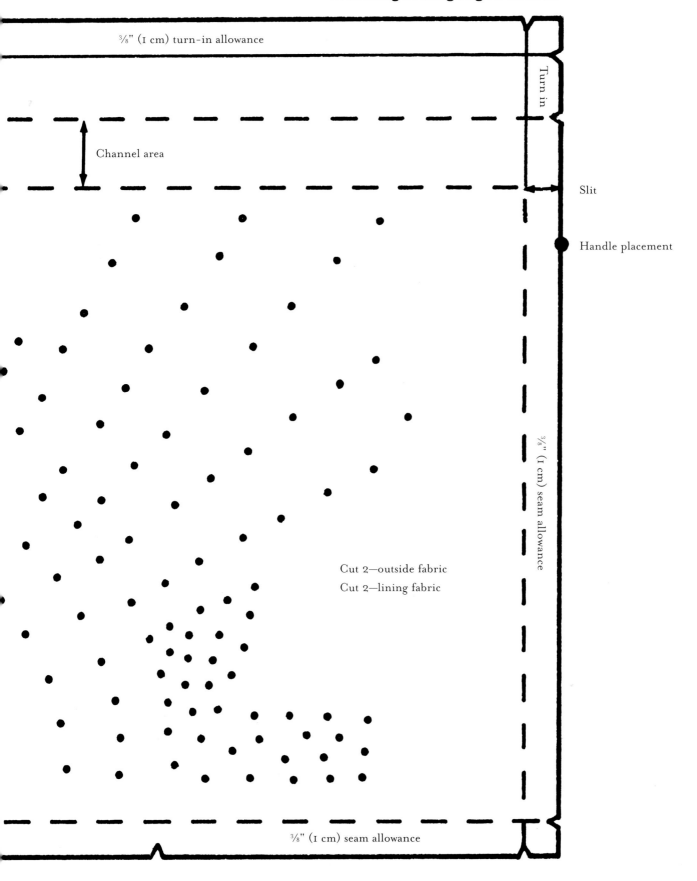

⅜" (1 cm) turn-in allowance

Turn in

Channel area

Slit

Handle placement

⅜" (1 cm) seam allowance

Cut 2—outside fabric
Cut 2—lining fabric

⅜" (1 cm) seam allowance

Beach Bag Pocket

Photocopy at 200%

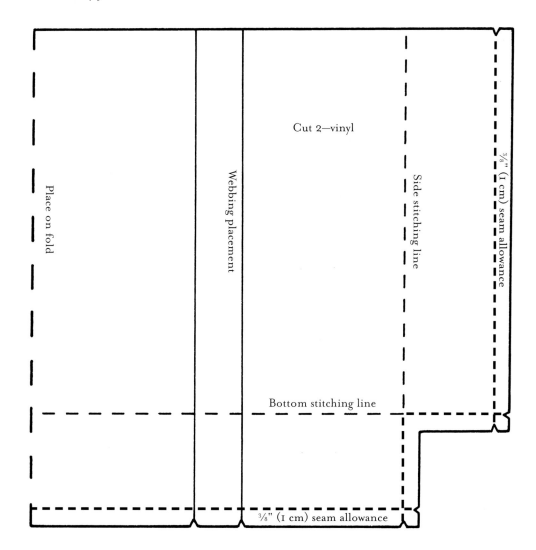

Cut 2—vinyl

Place on fold

Webbing placement

Side stitching line

³⁄₈" (1 cm) seam allowance

Bottom stitching line

³⁄₈" (1 cm) seam allowance

Clutch Bag Front/Back

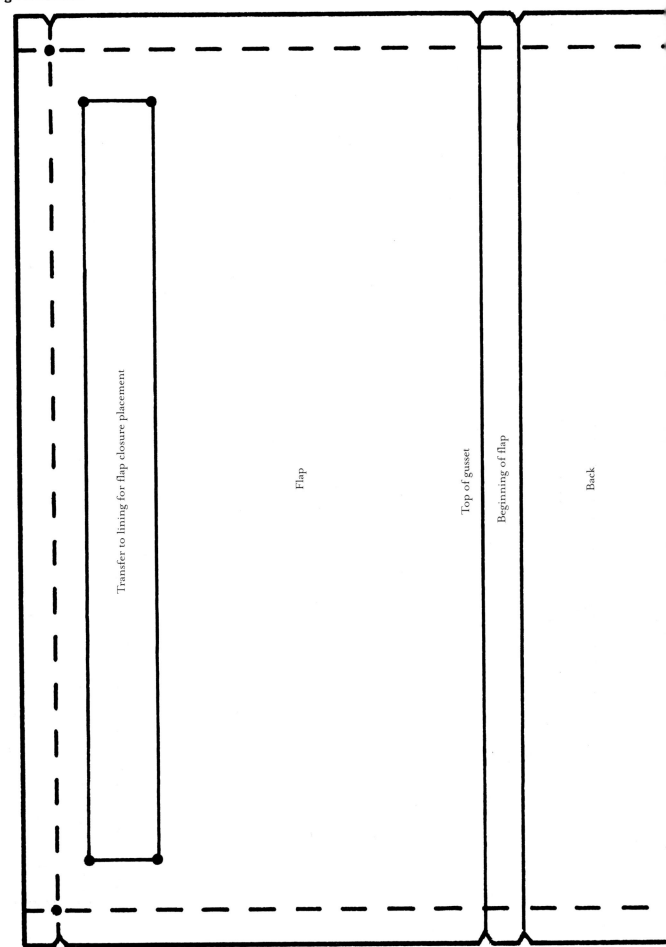

Transfer to lining for flap closure placement

Flap

Top of gusset

Beginning of flap

Back

auxiliary patterns

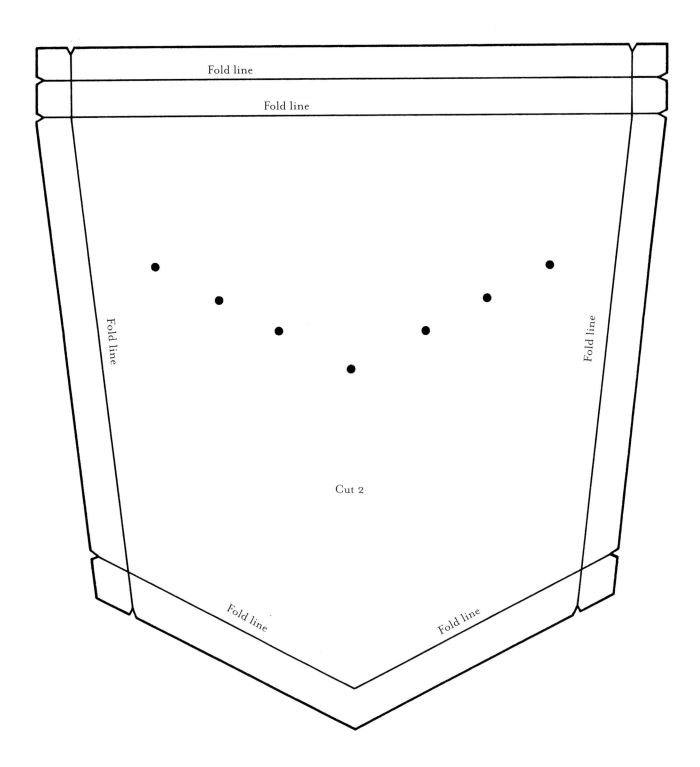

Fold line

Fold line

Fold line

Fold line

Cut 2

Fold line

Fold line

Mini Bridal Tote Bag Front/Back

Stop sewing cording here.
Stop sewing cording here.
3/8" (1 cm) turn-in allowance
1/8" (0.3 cm) satin ribbon
1/2" (1.3 cm) organza ribbon
3/8" (1 cm) bridal trim
1/2" (1.3 cm) organza ribbon
1/8" (0.3 cm) satin ribbon
Pearl
1/8" (0.3 cm) satin ribbon
1/2" (1.3 cm) organza ribbon
3/8" (1 cm) bridal trim
1/2" (1.3 cm) organza ribbon
1/8" (0.3 cm) satin ribbon
Cut 2—satin
Cut 2—lining fabric
Cut 2—felt or quilt batting
(without top 3/8" [1 cm] turn-in allowance)
3/8" (1 cm) seam allowance

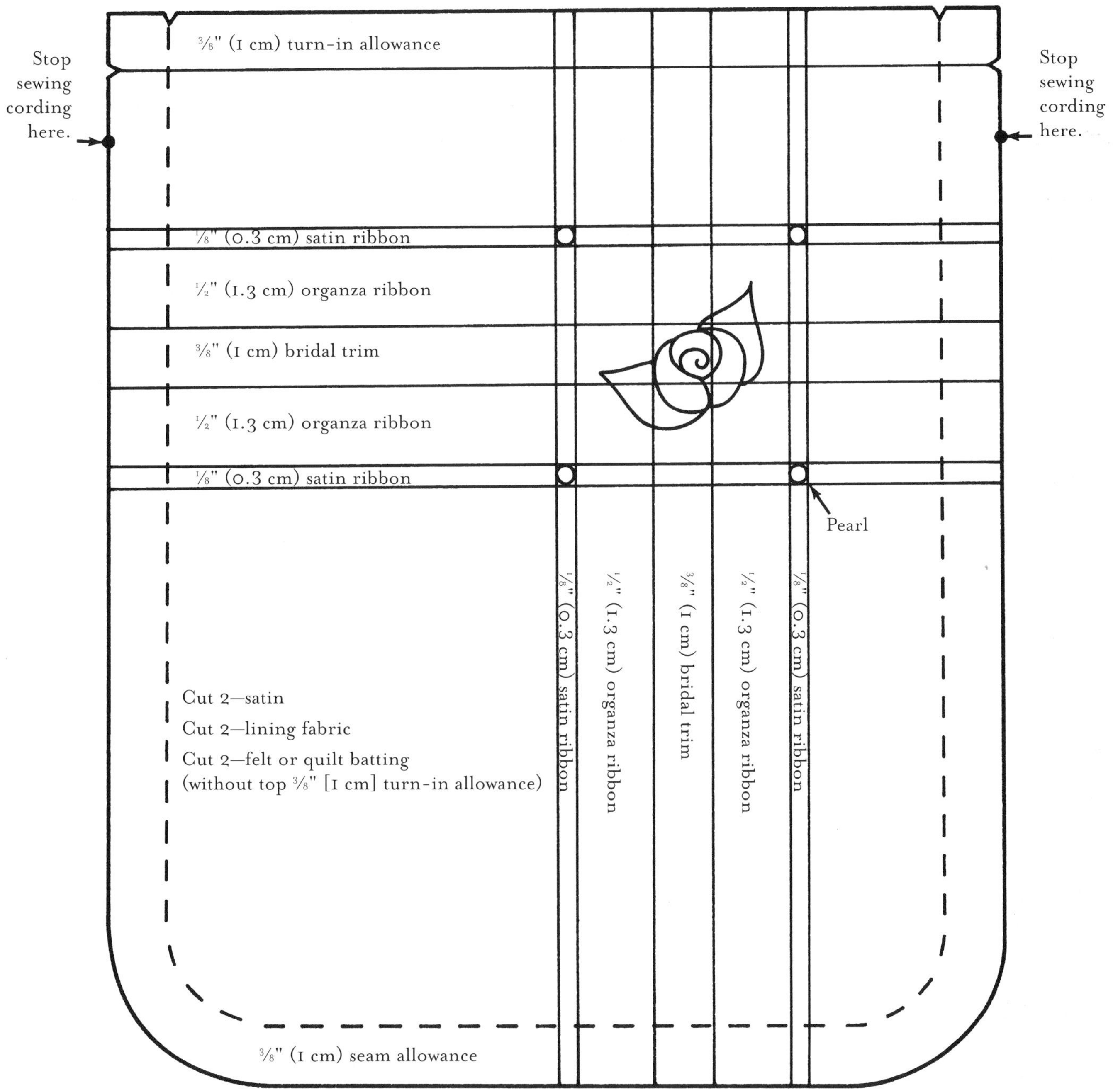

Mini Bridal Tote Bag Bottom/Gusset

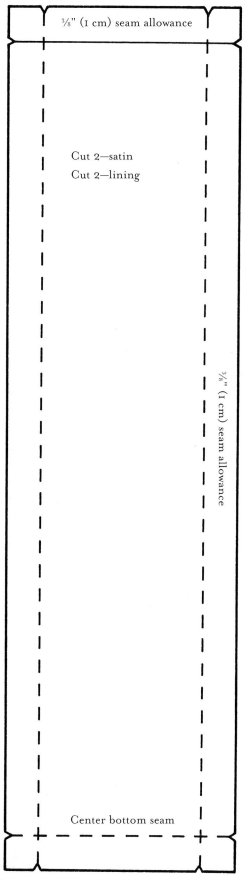

⅜" (1 cm) seam allowance

Cut 2—satin
Cut 2—lining

⅜" (1 cm) seam allowance

Center bottom seam

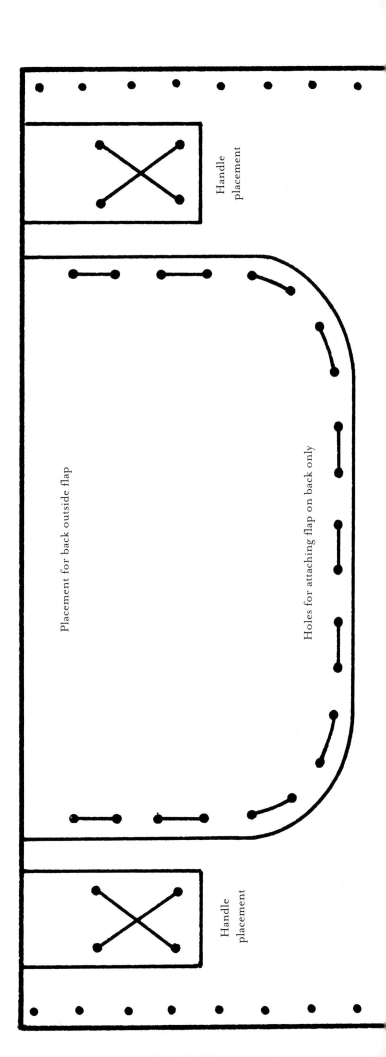

Handle placement

Placement for back outside flap

Holes for attaching flap on back only

Handle placement

Holes for button

Cut 2—leather

Holes to lace on bottom and gusset pieces

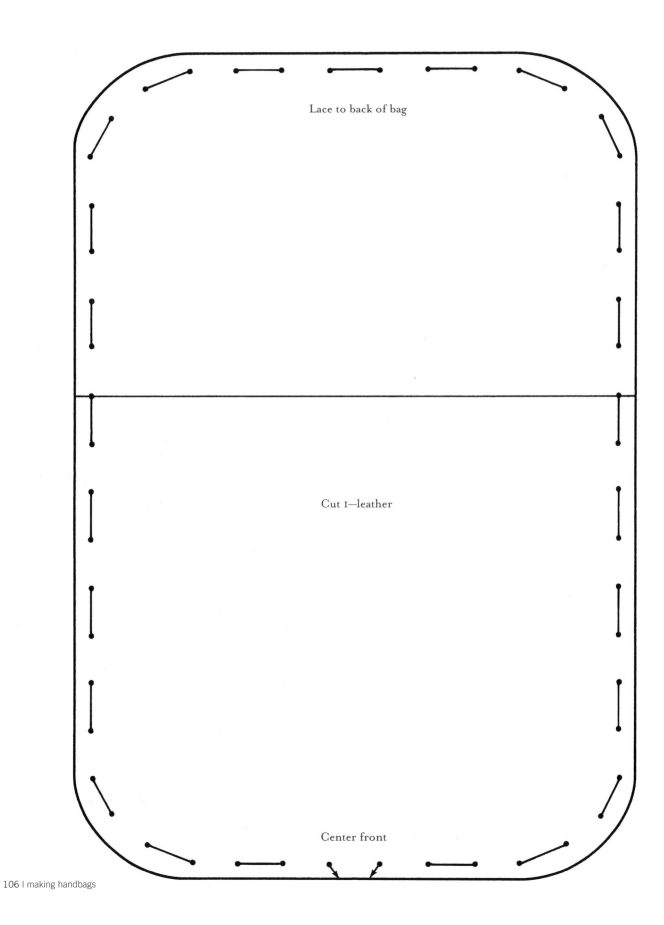

Lace to back of bag

Cut 1—leather

Center front

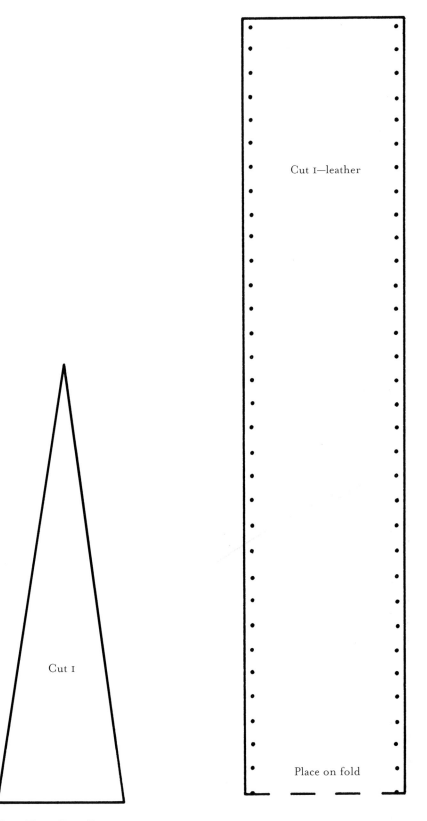

Cut I—leather

Place on fold

Cut I

Edge-Laced Leather Tote Bag Button

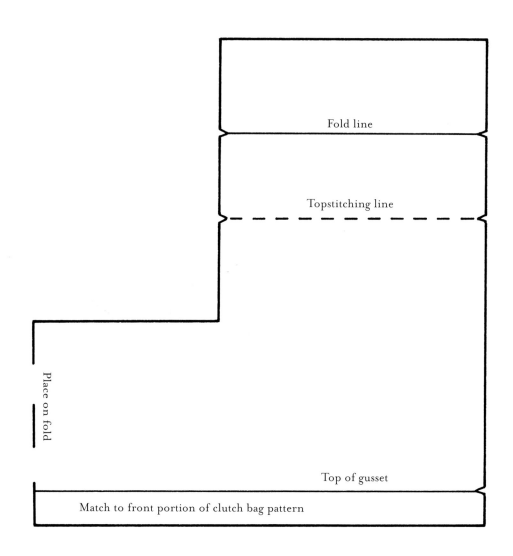

Fold line

Topstitching line

Place on fold

Top of gusset

Match to front portion of clutch bag pattern

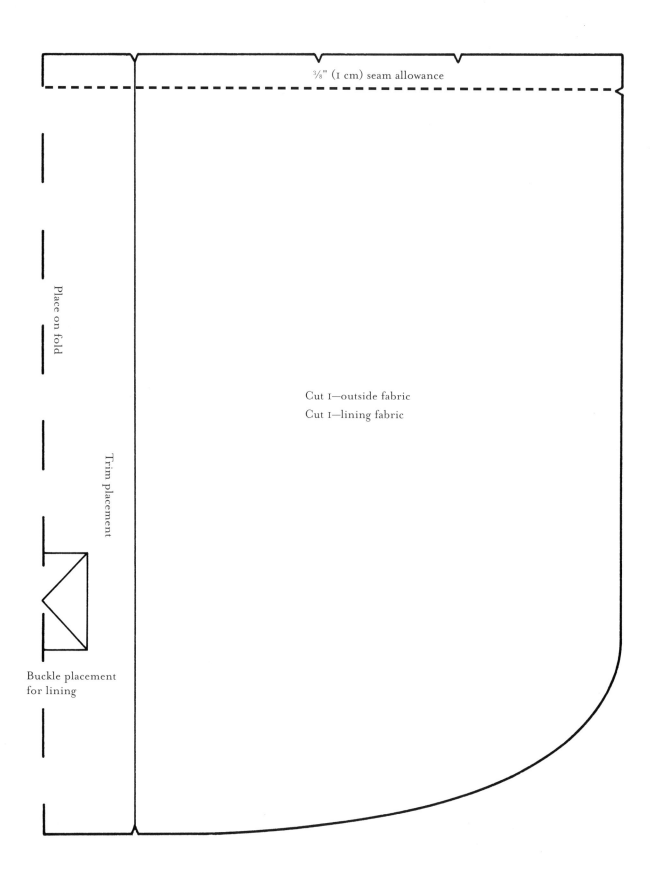

⅜" (1 cm) seam allowance

Place on fold

Trim placement

Cut 1—outside fabric
Cut 1—lining fabric

Buckle placement
for lining

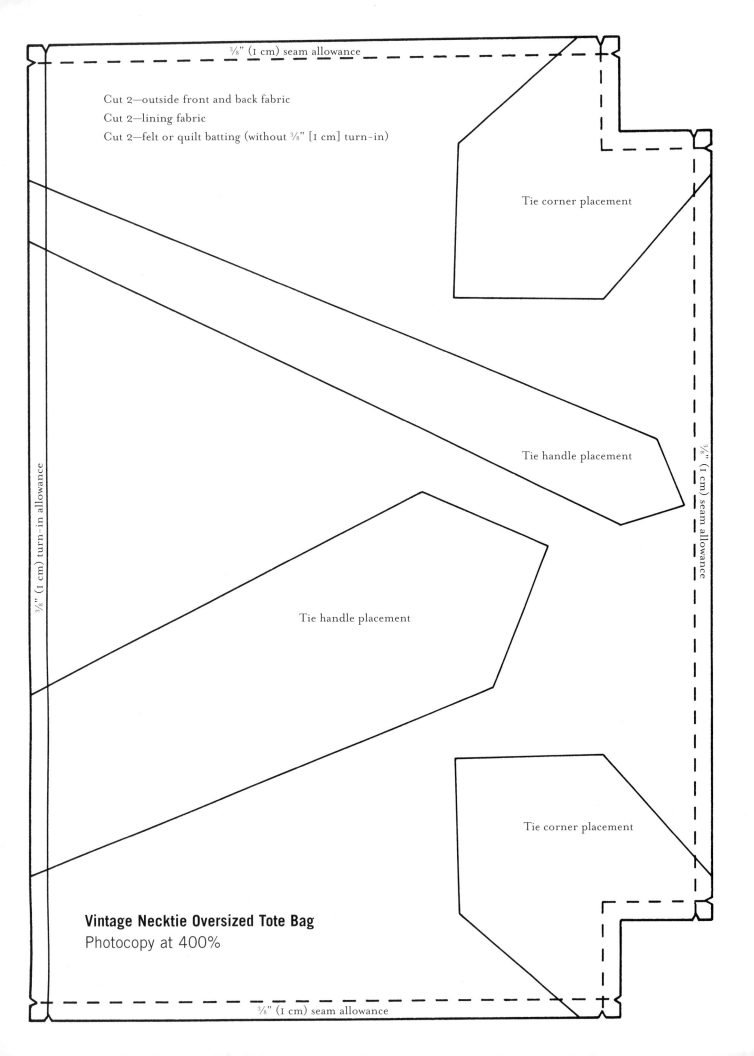

⅜" (1 cm) seam allowance

Cut 2—outside front and back fabric
Cut 2—lining fabric
Cut 2—felt or quilt batting (without ⅜" [1 cm] turn-in)

Tie corner placement

Tie handle placement

⅜" (1 cm) turn-in allowance

⅜" (1 cm) seam allowance

Tie handle placement

Tie corner placement

Vintage Necktie Oversized Tote Bag
Photocopy at 400%

⅜" (1 cm) seam allowance

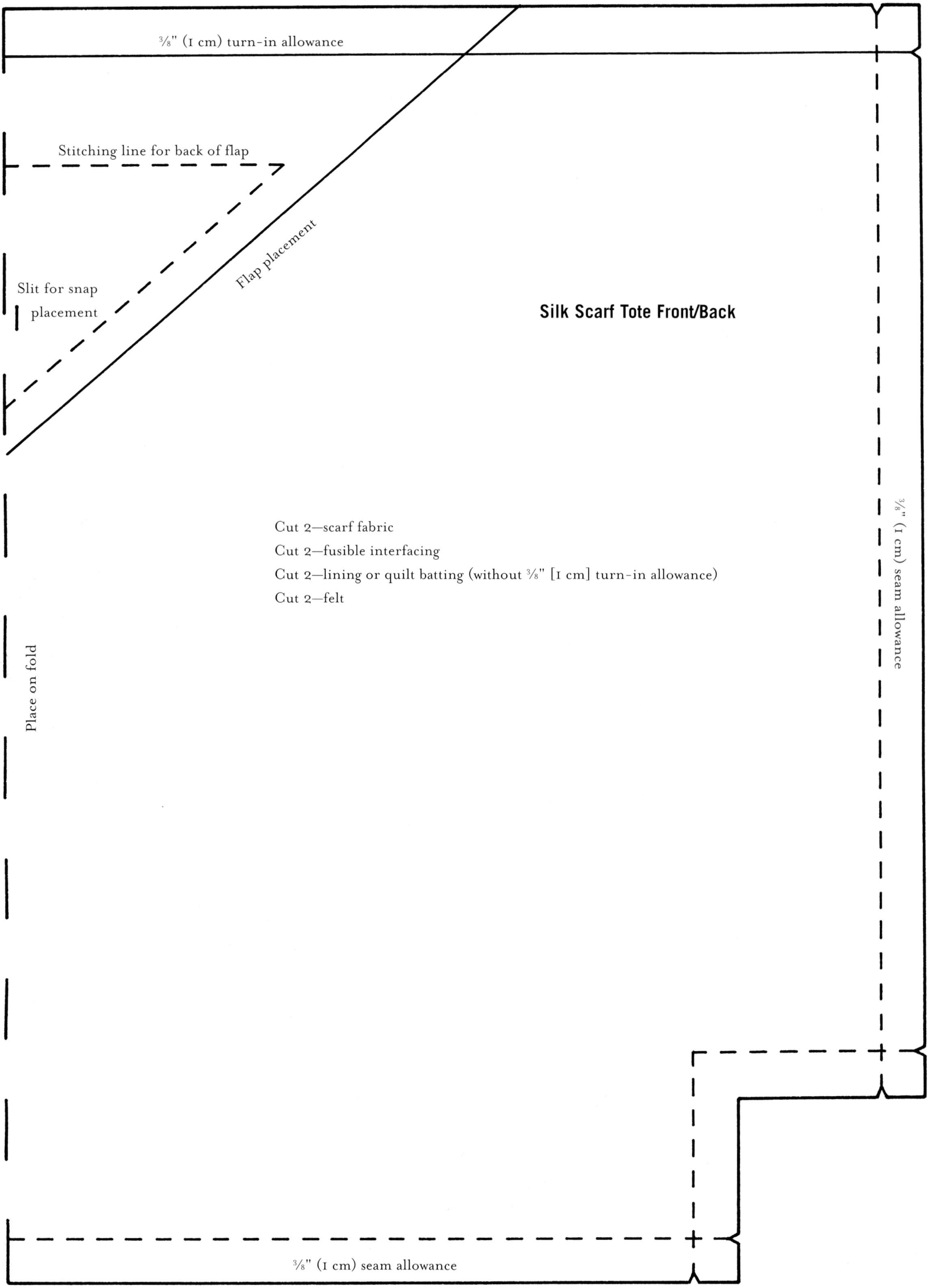

⅜" (1 cm) turn-in allowance

Stitching line for back of flap

Flap placement

Slit for snap placement

Silk Scarf Tote Front/Back

⅜" (1 cm) seam allowance

Cut 2—scarf fabric
Cut 2—fusible interfacing
Cut 2—lining or quilt batting (without ⅜" [1 cm] turn-in allowance)
Cut 2—felt

Place on fold

⅜" (1 cm) seam allowance

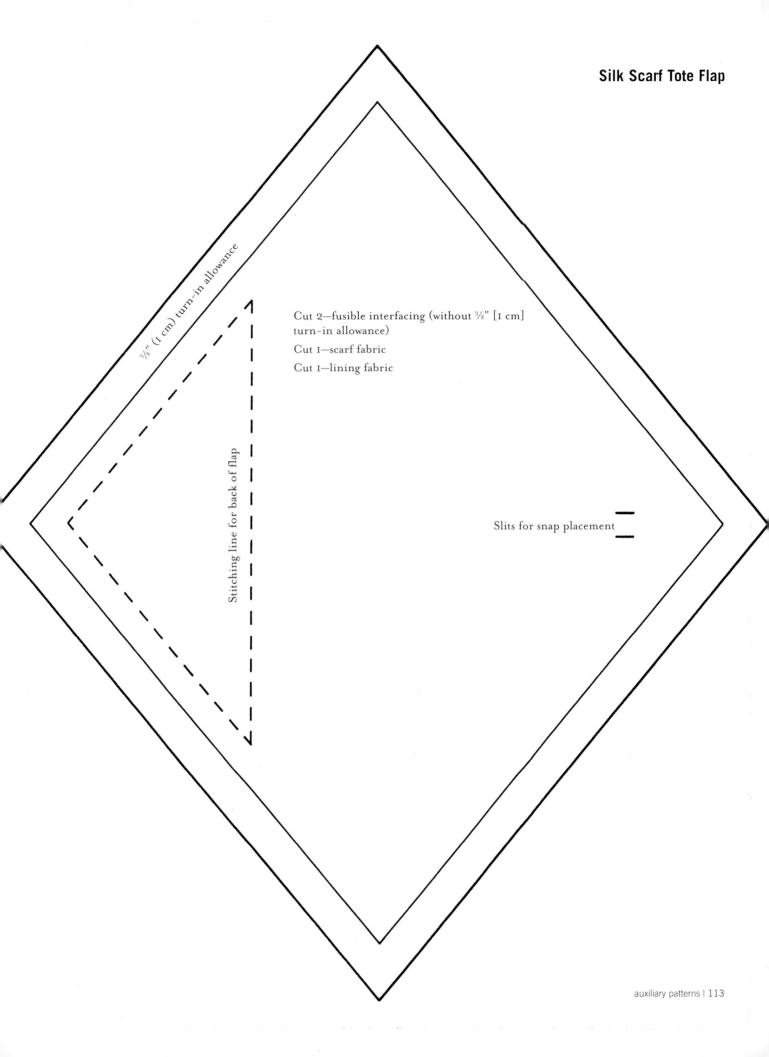

⅜" (1 cm) turn-in allowance

Cut 2—fusible interfacing (without ⅜" [1 cm] turn-in allowance)

Cut 1—scarf fabric

Cut 1—lining fabric

Stitching line for back of flap

Slits for snap placement

resources

A.C. Moore
www.acmoore.com
Nationwide Locations
(Arts and crafts supplies)

Active Trimming Co.
250 W. 39th St.
New York, NY 10018
(800) 878-6336
Catalog available

Art Station
144 W. 27th St.
New York, NY 10001
(212) 807-8000
www.artstationltd.com
(Arts and crafts supplies)

Atlanta Thread & Supply Co.
695 Red Oak Rd.
Stockbridge, GA 30281
(800) 847-1001
(Notions)
Catalog available

Brewer Sewing Supplies
3800 W. 42nd St.
Chicago, IL 60632
(800) 444-3111
(Sewing supplies)

Charm Woven Labels
2400 W. Magnolia Blvd.
Burbank, CA 91506
(800) 843-1111
www.charmwoven.com
(Woven labels)
Catalog available

Clotilde
2 Sew Smart Way, B8031
Stevens Pt., WI 54481-8031
(800) 772-2891
(Fabrics, sewing notions, and tools)
Catalog available

The Fabric & Fiber Sourcebook
Published by *Threads* Magazine
Mail-order guide

The Fabric Mill
168C Glen Cove Rd.
Carle Place, NY 11514
(516) 248-8799
(Fabrics and sewing notions)

Hansol Sewing Machine Co., Inc.
101 W. 26th St.
New York, NY 10001
(800) 463-9661
(Sewing machines)

Heal's
(stores in London, Kingston, Guildford)
Head Office
196 Tottenham Court Road
London W1T 7LQ
+44 (0)20 7636 1666
www.heals.com
(fabrics)

Herrschners
(800) 441-0838
(Sewing and craft supplies, fabrics)
Catalog available

HobbyCraft
(stores nationwide)
Head office
Bournemouth, United Kingdom
01202 596100
(Craft supplies)

JoAnn Fabrics
(888) 739-4120
www.joann.com
Nationwide locations
(Craft supplies, fabrics, and trimmings)
Catalog and magazine available

John Lewis
(stores nationwide)
Head office
Oxford Street
London W1A 1EX
+44 (06)20 7269 7711
www.johnlewis.co.uk
(Fabrics)

M & J Trimming
1008 6th Ave.
New York, NY
(212) 391-9072
(Trimmings)

Michael's Arts & Crafts
www.michaels.com
Nationwide Locations
(Arts and crafts supplies)

C.S. Osborne Tools
125 Jersey St.
Harrison, NJ 07029
(973) 483-3232
(Tools)
Catalog available

Pearl Paint
www.pearlpaint.com
Nationwide Locations
(Craft supplies)
Catalog available

Rose Brand
517 W. 35th St.
New York, NY 10001
(800) 223-1624
(Fabrications, fabrics, and theatrical supplies)

Selfridges
(stores in London and Manchester)
Head office
400 Oxford Street
London W1A 1AB
+44 (0)20 629 1234
(Fabrics)

Tandy Leather & Crafts
(800) 555-3130
www.tandyleather.com
(Crafting tools, leather, and suede)
Catalog available

Toho Shoji, Inc.
990 Sixth Ave.
New York, NY 10018
(212) 868-7465
(Buttons, chains, and trims)

Universal Mercantile Exchange, Inc.
13200 Brooks Dr. #E
Baldwin Park, CA 91706
(800) 921-5523
www.umei.com
(Buckles, buttons, chains, fasteners, handles, ornaments, and trims)
Catalog available

Veteran Leather
36-14 35th St.
Long Island City, NY 11106
(718) 786-9000
(Leather and suede)
Catalog available

Westphal & Co.
105 W. 30th St.
New York, NY 10001
(212) 563-5990
(Tools)
Catalog available

Zucker Feather Products
P.O. Box 331, 512 N. East St.
California, MO 65018
(573) 796-2183
Catalog available

contributors

NATIONAL ORGANIZATIONS

American Craft Council
72 Spring St.
New York, NY 10012
(212) 274-0630
Magazine available

American Sewing Guild
P.O. Box 8476
Medford, OR 98504
(503) 772-4059

National Craft Association
1945 E. Ridge Rd., Ste. 5178
Rochester, NY 14622-24671
(800) 715-9594
ncs@craftassoc.com

SCHOOLS AND COLLEGES

Cordwainers College
182 Mare St.
London E8 3RE
0181-985-0273
www.cordwainers.ac.uk
(Courses and degrees in handbag construction)

Fashion Institute of Technology
227 W. 27th St.
New York, NY 10001
(212) 217-7253
www.fitnyc.suny.edu
(Courses and degrees in accessories design)

Parsons School of Design
66 Fifth Ave.
New York, NY 10011
(212) 741-8668
(Courses in handbag construction)

All gallery contributors are students from the accessories design department at theFashion Institute of Technology, New York, New York, Class of 2002.

Jury Artola
South Beach, Florida
miany83@yahoo.com

Samantha Chère Beckerman
Toronto, Canada
samanthachere@hotmail.com

Veronica Cajucom
New York, New York
ivyfaye@hotmail.com

Yi Jen Chen
Ti Pei, Taiwan
kittymao-chan@yahoo.com

Cheryl Greenblatt
New York, New York
cjgreenblatt@nyc.rr.com or
maizeeg@village.com

Celina Guity
Bay Island, Roatan, Honduras
celiguity@yahoo.com

Keeva Halferty
New York, New York
keevais@hotmail.com

Kelly Herron
Massapequa, New York
kelleykennedyny@aol.com

Ines Kim
Korea
inessita@aol.com

Rika Maeda
Osaka, Japan
rika_maeda@yahoo.com

Mokgadi Matlhako
Pretoria, South Africa
ladyoffashion@hotmail.com

Cary Mitsi Nomiyama
New York, New York
mtznomi@aol.com

Linda Diane Polichetti
New York, New York
lpolic@hotmail.com

Jessica Todd
Medford, New Jersey
buggirl321@aol.com

Erendira Tristan
Guadalajara, Mexico
e_tristan@yahoo.com

Jaymie Stroud
Kansas
jastroud@yahoo.com

Katharine M. Wall
Westchester, New York
party4kit@aol.com

about the authors

ELLEN GOLDSTEIN-LYNCH is the chairperson of the accessories design department at the Fashion Institute of Technology in New York. She has been involved in the accessories field for more than 25 years. For ten years she has served as public relations director for the National Fashion Accessories Association. She is an authority on handbags and accessories and has been featured on national television and in print.

SARAH MULLINS is a graduate and faculty member of the accessories design department at the Fashion Institute of Technology in New York. Sarah does freelance design for several New York–based companies and also has her own line of unique handbags. Her passion is experimenting with different combinations of materials in her designs.

NICOLE MALONE is an accessories designer with a zeal for handbags. She has freelance experience in pattern making, sample making, and construction of one-of-a-kind creations for various handbag and fashion designers. A graduate of the accessories design program at the Fashion Institute of Technology in New York, she currently designs and produces her own line of handbags and belts under the name Stargon Accessories. But her true love is teaching in the accessories design department at her alma mater.

acknowledgments

ELLEN GOLDSTEIN-LYNCH

To Jim, Thomas, Brandon, Janis, Little Brandon, and Hoolie, who are the light of my life. To Gale Keenan, buds forever. Special kudos to the dynamic group of students, faculty, and friends with whom I share my life at FIT.

Thanks to Mary Ann and Rockport Publishers for pitching this book to us. To Nicole and Sarah, thanks for letting me be as creative as you guys. It was a blast! And to Dr. John Marino; without him, I would not be here today.

SARAH MULLINS

I would like to thank the entire FIT faculty and staff and its students for endlessly teaching me about handbag design. Three cheers for Alex, my family, and my friends (especially Dan and Maureen), who have constant words of encouragement and who are always willing to wear my creations. Thank you Nicole, Ellen, and Mary Ann for making this book such a pleasure to work on.

NICOLE MALONE

To my former instructors and present-day colleagues at FIT, who have taught me so much over the years. To all my students, who never cease to amaze me! To all my friends, especially Sarah, without whom I'd be lost. To the love of my life, Kevin. To my family (all the Shnozzys) and especially my mom and dad, who have done so much for me: I love you!